JOLENE MERCADANTE

The Angel on My Shoulder

My Life with an American Pit Bull Terrier

iUniverse, Inc.
Bloomington

The Angel on My Shoulder
My Life with an American Pit Bull Terrier

iUniverse books may be ordered through booksellers or by contacting:

iUniverse
1663 Liberty Drive
Bloomington, IN 47403
www.iuniverse.com
1-800-Authors (1-800-288-4677)

ISBN: 978-1-4620-2761-3 (sc)
ISBN: 978-1-4620-2762-0 (hc)
ISBN: 978-1-4620-2763-7 (e)

Library of Congress Control Number: 2011909306

Printed in the United States of America

iUniverse rev. date: 10/27/2011

*To Lily, the sweetest soul with whom
I've ever and will ever have been blessed
to share my life. I know at least one angel
was waiting with open wings.*

'Tis mine to be in love with life,
And mine to hear the Robins sing;
'Tis mine to live apart from strife,
And kneel to flowers blossoming –
    To all things fair,
    As at a shine –
    To drink the air
    As I would wine.
To Love I've built a temple here,
Beneath the boughs of oak and pine,
Beside a spring that all the year
Tells of a harmony divine.
    I own no creeds
    Sweet Love beside –
    My spirit's needs
    Are satisfied.

Nature's Blessings, Alex Posey

Acknowledgements

There are so many who have supported me in my journey. Without them, I doubt I would have had the strength to persevere.

First and foremost, to Rumer, who changed my life in the most profound way and gave me the gift of our story.

My family, both the Mercadantes and Perottis, for their most generous love and support.

To every single person who attended my first book talk on August 3, 2009 before my book was even published! That night, the power of love and positive collectedness was revealed.

Pat Leveille, for her gift of "Puppy Angel" and who lent me her ear so often, it now probably hangs loose.

Paula Harrison, who opened the door by helping me conquer my fear.

Dr. John Perdrizet, our human angel, without whom our lives wouldn't be complete.

Doctors Schlaffers and LaRocca, all of whom made a point of being there in Rumer's need.

My two Wendys, Wendy McAnanama and Wendy Perotti, the first who propelled me on my way and the second who keeps me true, and, both of whom offer the unfailing support of true sisters.

Carolyn Schwartz, my editor. You took the weight of the world off my shoulders. I will forever be indebted to you for your kindness and willingness to take on this project.

And, Cheryl... I know if I've said it once, I've said it a million times, "What would I ever do without you?"

Introduction

Rumer's story has chased me these last six years, my deep desire to write her story overshadowed by the pain of her loss. I thought of my title and began the first page three years ago where it sat until now, when I truly started in earnest, to put it all together. At first, it was too painful—the hole she left in all our lives much too deep. In order to write, I had to let myself feel this pain again; it was so heavy in my heart that the pressure was almost unbearable. So, I ran.

Eventually, I found that I could only accept such cowardice from myself for so long. The wisp of memory, of Rumer's strength and bravery, her beauty and generosity, finally caught me. It brushed me with such power that I felt the shame of my escape… I began to write.

As I wrote, I soon realized I had another fear: would I be able to convey, to the depth I desired, the almost 13 years of my life spent with her? Would I be able to convey how much she meant, how we began our lives together, how she grew up from that tiny perfect little puppy to that splendid adult, her personality, her funniness, her gentle sweetness? For me, the things that fade with time are the hardest part of losing someone. Can I remember them enough, the way they looked, the way they walked, the way they smelled, the little parts and quirks of their character that made them who they were, the way they felt in my arms when I hugged them so tightly with love? Sometimes I really have to calm myself while thinking about the extinction of these memories. It's as if they were carved out of my mind, one by one, like endangered species disappearing from Earth. Once they are gone they will never return, and that is what makes the loss so devastating.

The fear of knowing that my memories of Rumer were dwindling propelled me forward. Sometimes the loss of painful memories and the passage of time are blessings, helping us to heal. In this particular instance, time proved to be a thief: stealing my memories, my treasures, my most precious possessions. Even the pain that went along with them was an essential part of my soul, and I jealously held everything close to my heart. If I lost them, I lost essential pieces of my being, my core, my essence, all of me that was shaped so tenderly, so lovingly, so "goodly" by living them.

On a more pragmatic level, I was also passionately driven to write this book to address the constant threat of breed specific legislation, or BSL, especially in Massachusetts in 2007. Faced with the possibility of choosing between moving or having my dogs euthanized, this book became imperative. In 2004, a ban was passed in Denver that caused pit bulls to be confiscated and euthanized even if they were family pets. And, as usual, the responsible, honest, and honorable dog owners are held to the punishment while the "underground" world of dog fighting and dog abuse goes on.

Standing up for these dogs' rights became a moral and ethical calling for me. Many pit bulls are victims of so much abuse and torture that they sometimes are turned against their very sweet nature. Contrary to stereotypes, the American Pit Bull Terrier has been bred throughout its history to be human-friendly; the human- aggressive gene is actually bred out of them. It takes much damage, either to the breeding stock or to the dog itself, to turn them into dangerous animals. Many end up in shelters, found abandoned on the streets by the thousands because they are simply unable to comply with abusers who wish to turn them aggressive. It would serve everyone's best interest to prosecute the criminals who are doing the abusing rather than these tormented innocents who endure abuses that include hanging, electrocuting, being blown up, or becoming the "bait" with which the fighters are trained, torn apart piece by painful piece.

In addition to rescue work, I help these dogs in as many other ways as possible. I give money to pit bull causes. I write to anyone who spreads misinformation on the breed, denigrates them in some way, or doesn't look upon them as feeling, living creatures, such as PETA, certain television news anchors, and a few authors. I write to encourage those who show pit bulls in a good light, like author Cody McFadyen. *Sports Illustrated* finally made amends for its terrible article on pit bulls in the '80s by recently featuring a most beautiful article on the Michael Vick dogs. The show *L.A. Ink*, Old Navy commercials, National Geographic Channel, Best Friends Organization /Dogtown, and Cesar Millan are all very positive influences on the image of pit bulls. I thank Mr. Millan every day for saving so many lives that others have given up on. His show has been responsible for changing countless people's opinions on pit bulls with help from his own dogs, Daddy and Junior. I also send letters to state legislators and senators whenever necessary. I finally registered to vote, and this was the only issue that could get me to do so.

I find it difficult to keep up with the letters that need to be written against the injustices toward these dogs. This book has become my effort, another way I can somehow help. Helping these dogs has become my cause and my purpose. It's a passion born out of my love for animals in general, the unfairness of societal views toward pit bulls specifically, and my personal love for the gentle sweetness that is the American Pit Bull Terrier.

At night Cheryl and I often look at our two, snoring in bed, cuddled together, so comfortable and happy with their lives, oblivious to any other way, and often think, "Where would they have ended up?" In bed, we talk quietly together and laugh about things the dogs might have done that day, always coming back to the same questions: "Who would understand these two as we do?"…"What would we ever do without them?"… "What would they do without each other?"

Recent events such as Michael Vick's crime make me wonder and make my heart ache. I look at my angels and think, "It could have been you." Our little Mei Mei, who would rather kiss us than eat, could have been a "bait" dog for fighting practice, torn to shreds over and over in an endless nightmare until death brings release. Our Aderyn Hale, so beautiful inside and out that we call her Aderyn Halo, could have been chosen as a fighter. After revealing her true good spirit, she would have been strangled with bare hands, hung, electrocuted, or had her brains blown out in disgust. A lover instead of a fighter, her beloved, precious body would have been discarded like trash.

The only good thing to have come out of the Michael Vick situation is that it has alerted people to the horrible ways in which these dogs are abused. It has made people see that these dogs need our help. Communities are starting to realize that we must make irresponsible owners take responsibility for their dogs no matter the breed, for any creature can be tortured to insanity. Many legislators are beginning to see this as the correct choice rather than breed-specific bans, which are proven to be ineffective. Even the Dutch government has recently lifted its 25-year ban on pit bulls, realizing that this is not the solution.

"It's only a dog" or "It's only an animal" or "They're here on earth for man to dominate and do as he will anyway"... How I detest these words, the meaning, the philosophy behind them. How are we ever supposed to be kinder and less aggressive with each other if we cannot have kindness toward animals, the most innocent (along with children) creatures on earth? How are we ever going to make it as a species, both physically and spiritually? People have such misconceptions about animals: they don't feel pain like we do; they are not as intelligent; they cannot reason; they are inferior to humans...all in order to feel better about how we treat them. Something has to be done about animal abuse. We have to start raising our children with kindness and consideration in their hearts. As Gandhi said, "The greatness of a nation and its moral progress can be judged by the way its animals are treated." We need to try much harder to aspire to those words if we are to pass that kind of judgment.

After my Rumer died and we found Aderyn Hale, we wished to get her a sister when she turned one. We researched to see if this would be a possibility, not wanting two dogs that couldn't get along. We read things like: "Don't ever leave your pit bull alone with your cat" or "Don't leave your pit bulls alone together, they'll tear each other apart." This almost stopped us from getting our little Mei Mei Olivia. Thankfully, we found those few websites and had those few friends who said differently. Although many aren't as lucky, our dogs are now soul mates and the two of them are always left alone together, along with my 18-year-old cat.

I could write a whole book just on my Aderyn and Mei, how smart they are, how sensitive they are, how manipulating, how they have the ability to think and reason. To have them in my life is an honor, yet I'm mindful of the responsibility I have in owning pit bulls. Because my dogs are the breed they are, I know they would be blamed for something, whether or not it was their fault. Even something as simple as obtaining homeowner's insurance can be a challenge due to the prejudice against this breed. Many people are denied insurance if they have a pit bull, and those who are approved are often forced to pay an exorbitant price. It makes me endeavor to live every day of my life with my dogs as an example of what the true pit bull is.

Because of my pit bulls, I've changed the opinions of co-workers, family members, and people I meet by telling stories about them. I recount how they kiss, how they respect my 18-year-old cat and two horses, how my mother "babysits" them during the week, and on and on...all such normal stories about normal dogs, not monsters. Just recently, a co-worker told me that he loves pit bulls but believes a lot of the negative feelings toward them stem from their "locking jaws." I had to explain to him that this is a terrible myth. Pit bulls do not have locking jaws. They don't even have the most powerful jaws of the different dog breeds. Was he surprised!

If nothing else, Rumer's story reveals both her beautiful life and the way she touched so many others with her positive, life-changing influence. I'm not going to lie or exaggerate the facts, for Rumer did have her "faults." She loved rolling in deer and goose poop, she loved going through the trash, she was agoraphobic, she took advantage of every situation, and she barked to an annoying degree. She may not have been a heroic rescue dog, therapy dog, war hero, valued police dog, or agility star. There are many other pit bulls who can claim the fame for all of these things, and more. Though she only affected lives in our small world, she *was* all of these things to us...she *did* save us, she *did* rescue us, and she *was* our hero in so many ways. Rumer was an ordinary dog in an ordinary life, but so extraordinary for that.

So, that wisp of Rumer's ghost lightly brushing my back as I ran away was cajoling, reminding me of how much her story *needed* to be told. It brought me to a screeching halt. She made me realize in the most profound way that her story shatters the pit bull myths, the horrible stereotypes. If it can alter one legislator's vote, change one person's opinion, bring one abuser to justice, or save one life, I know Rumer would be happy. And all those dogs killed due to ignorance might be able to rest a little easier, a little more at peace.

When I sometimes tire, either in the pursuit of publishing or in the pursuit for justice, Cheryl will remind me, "Did Rumer ever let any obstacles get in her way? Every day, she got up and went on, despite all the obstacles she faced. She had cancer, was barely able to walk, bloated to almost twice her weight...she still went on, and went on happily. No, her obstacles never stopped her."

So, Rumer keeps me strong and always will. I try to be true, I try to be as honest about what she was, what she meant, what she's done for me in my life. I would never want to dishonor her by thinking more of her than she was. If anything, I believe the dishonor is done by the lack of words strong enough to demonstrate the impact she had.

To not write her story, to not reveal to people how beautiful and pure an American Pit Bull Terrier has made all our lives, would be a dire affront to her memory. My conscience supplied the will, but the inspiration came from the divine, my Angel Pie.

Prologue

It was a brisk October evening when Cheryl's quick steps approached the dimly-lit house in North Adams, Massachusetts. A slight breeze blew the dry, crackling leaves in a circular swirl around her feet and then stilled. She hesitated, nervously glancing up at the clear night sky, the stars like bright diamonds, glittering in the fall blackness. Although nervous, determination to hear her fate overpowered her unease.

She squared her shoulders and began walking once again, sneakers crunching along the stone walkway, approaching the entry of the old house. A woman opened the door, putting her hand out in greeting, "Cheryl?" she asked, "Please, come in."

The words Cheryl heard from this nationally known psychic would foreshadow all to come. For, years before she met me, years before Rumer entered our lives, the psychic's words bespoke our future together.

That evening, meeting the woman's kind gaze, Cheryl, suddenly at ease, smiled and stepped forward to meet the psychic's prediction without further uncertainty:

'You will have an unconventional marriage. You will both have a daughter and she will be very special and unique. She will be a teacher to the world, the public, and people will be drawn to her beauty and intelligence, in a most spiritual way.'

BEGINNING

The road to peace, love, and happiness is paved in many forms but sometimes it is literally just that: a plain, old-fashioned paved road. Why can't we appreciate the moments in time that change all that come after them, directing our paths in life to the point of no return, and, in my case, for so much the better? Why can't we recognize them and savor such moments before they're gone, forever out of our grasp, never to be relived again in quite the same way? Although I've traveled many other paths of peace, love, and happiness since, how I wish I could travel that road of February 1992 from Southampton to Amesbury, Massachusetts once again. Only this time, I would know to treasure, appreciate, and revere it every step of the way.

CHAPTER 1

The ad in the *Boston Globe* was simple: "Pit Bull puppies for sale. Parents on premises." After calling the number and getting directions, we were off on a 2 ½ hour ride from Southampton to Amesbury. As we walked quickly to the car, I glanced up in excitement at the icy blue February sky. Wispy clouds like feathers adorned the Easter-egg blue with their brilliant white. The bitter cold air was shut out of the car with an emphatic slam as Cheryl and I jumped in to begin our drive. We couldn't wait to see the puppies and chattered the whole way, wondering what the dogs would look like, about the puppy we would choose, so excited to pick our new baby out of the 2 ½ week-old litter.

When we reached the farm and pulled into the driveway, we were greeted by fifteen adult pit bulls chained to doghouses in the yard, out of reach of each other by just a few feet. They eagerly began inquisitive barking, some of them leaping straight up in the air excitedly against their collars as we rolled to a stop in front of the house. With little knowledge about pit bulls going in, I curiously studied them, amazed at their variety of colors and looks. Cheryl was afraid of dogs and wouldn't leave the car, so I opened the driver's side door and stepped out alone. Even with the din of barking, no one came out to greet us. I approached the side door of the quaint house, sneakers crunching in the snow, zipping my coat and hunching my shoulders to the cold.

As I knocked, I couldn't help but look in the window of the door. To my surprise, I met the eyes of the most beautiful dog I had ever seen. He was standing in the kitchen, watching me with keen intelligence. There was no barking, just a steady stare from curious brown eyes. His body was a deep auburn and his face had the chiseled beauty of a classic pit bull, almost human in its shape, his ears cropped. He stood as still and soundless as air. His gaze stayed on me as a man approached the doorway.

"Hello, there," came a friendly Yankee accent from a big, burly, surprisingly young farmer. As he introduced himself as Wade, I couldn't help but comment on the beauty of the dog inside.

"This is Teddy Bear," Wade said as I stepped into the house. "He isn't one that I've bred, but one I've taken in." He explained that he was also the dog officer in town.

Teddy Bear was not only beautiful, but was extremely friendly, wiggling and rubbing against me as I scratched his back. His tail was docked, which Wade told me was highly unusual and only done because the person who had owned him kept him inside and didn't want him knocking things over. "Normally though," he said, "pit bulls are admired for long, beautiful tails, the longer and more sloping the better."

After our greetings and some small talk, Wade asked me to follow him to the far side of the yard where all the puppy kennels were located. I waved for Cheryl to follow and she finally mustered up enough courage to come. As we meandered through the sea of chained adults, we were sniffed and licked vigorously by any tongue that could reach us. Cheryl and I felt nothing but good intentions from the dogs, and, faced with such a joyful welcome, Cheryl realized that she wasn't even afraid anymore.

I found that I just had to stop and pet these sweet dogs who vied so ardently for our attention. Not one was aggressive in any way and I commented on this fact to Wade. Having not had much experience with the breed other than the horror stories I had read, I had not known what to expect. Wade agreed and told us that, because of their nature and how friendly they were, his dogs had been stolen numerous times. That's why they were chained with thick locks on their collars. The chains were as thick as my forearms and their dragging had removed all of the grass from around each of the 15 doghouses. The dirt left behind was strewn with cow bones as big and as long as my thighs.

Wade stopped at one dog and told us that this was the father of the babies we would be choosing from. His name was Steamer, and he was just as beautiful as Teddy Bear but in different ways. He was a very light vanilla color, with black-rimmed eyes like milk chocolate and the shape of almonds, and a black nose. He was shorter and stockier where Teddy

Bear was taller and leaner. His muzzle was shorter and more full with the tip of his nose lifting just a bit. I kneeled in front of him and placed my hand on his massive head to pet him. He couldn't stop licking me as I stroked him. "He's beautiful!" I exclaimed, as his tongue stretched out desperately to reach my face, eyes crossed to meet mine. It made me laugh, such a display of complete love for a total stranger. His head was shaped like that of an elephant, with a deep ridge running down the center surrounded by jaws of pure muscle.

We left Steamer and continued toward the doghouses in the back amidst the pines. As we walked along the path that cut through the snow, Wade began to tell us a little history of the breed and named a few famous pit bulls like the dog in the "Little Rascals" television show and Helen Keller's companion and helper. We approached the kennels of the mother dogs and Wade continued, "As a breeder, I appreciate people like you so much who are interested in my dogs, good family people with whom these dogs deserve to live. It's so hard for me when people of questionable motives come to pick out my dogs. I try to do what I can to discourage them, but…" He shook his shoulders and put out his hands, palms up, in a sad gesture.

We finally made it, the journey toward our choice nearing its end as we reached the doghouses of the mother pit bulls. We noticed that each mother had her own fenced kennel area, half cement and half dirt. The areas were very neat, clean, and well-kept. Wade stopped at the first house and lifted one side of the top. Inside was a mother dog with many puppies about six weeks old. "These are all taken," Wade said, "but I just wanted to show you."

Inside the house it was roomy and warm, a heating pad covering the floor. Wade said, "I put heating pads in all of the whelping houses during the cold winter months. It just makes me feel better to know the little ones are warm." The mother dog watched carefully as we pet the wriggling mass below us.

A biting wind picked up as Wade took the top off the next house. A mother pit bull came jumping out, laughing the way only a pit bull can. She was a beautiful dark brindle, her shiny black coat lined like a zebra with orange and brown stripes, her feet a dainty white. She was much more feminine and had a very sweet face. Five little lumps were on the heating pad on the floor of the house. "This is Leigha," Wade said, "the mama."

I pet Leigha's head excitedly while leaning over as far as I could, trying to get my first look at those little babies as Wade reached down into the house. Out came his hands, a puppy in each palm. "These are the only two available. I'm keeping the rest from this litter."

We looked in his hands. In his left was a little brindle female, so much like her mother, and in his right was a little light red female with a full black muzzle. Cheryl and I looked them both over very carefully. They were so cute! In all of our planning, we had been drawn to the brindle dogs and had talked over picking out a brindle puppy, but the red one was so beautiful. She had a full black face and black-rimmed eyes just like her father. As we were going back and forth, Wade was telling us how it was much more difficult to place brindle pit bulls. He said they look scarier to people. We didn't think that little brindle the size of a sausage in Wade's palm could ever look scary!

It was so hard to choose and there were so many times since then that we wished we had taken both puppies. But, we immediately fell in love with the perfect little red sausage with the full black muzzle in Wade's right hand. After talking it over, we chose her and not Brenda, the brindle. "Okay," Wade said as he laughed happily with Cheryl and me, "I'll call you when she's ready to go. Her name is Chilli Pepper." Or, as he pronounced it, Chilli "Peppah".

Little did I realize how much that small, seemingly insignificant moment in time would change so many people and affect so many lives. Little did I know that I was beginning the journey of a lifetime, a journey that would teach me the greatest and most important things in life. This journey would change me spiritually and would change the very way I lived the rest of my life in thought, relationships, and love. It was a journey that was set in motion by this single little soul the size of a sausage.

After our choice, it was so hard to leave her. But, we pulled out of Wade's driveway and turned toward home, excitedly talking about this new little life and all she already meant. After a while, we fell silent, quietly lost in our own thoughts. As I drove, I thought about what brought me to this point and what my life with animals had taught me about love. I didn't yet realize that everything I thought I knew about love would be nothing compared to what I was about to learn.

CHAPTER 2

From my very first memorable thoughts, I have loved animals with a passion that can only be attributed to the innate. I loved animals so much that I wanted to be one. I crawled around our house as a child, pretending to be a dog, and barked at the sink for water. One of my sisters asked me, "Would you like a drink, Fifi?" Panting, I shook my head up and down, and barked again. One of them then retrieved my glass and tipped it just so for me to drink.

My childhood home was any child's dream. It had a beautiful yard complete with a pond and a brook that passed through, both of which hosted numerous fish, frogs, and creatures of the mud that kept me occupied all day long, happy as a pig and just as muddy. Playing one summer afternoon amongst all these wonderful creatures, I heard my mother call me in to take my daily nap. Without arguing, I dutifully trudged in and upstairs to my room, clutching my bright yellow plastic purse. With such obedience highly unusual, my mother followed quietly behind me. Peeking in the crack of the bedroom door, she smiled and held back a laugh as she watched me speak into my purse, turn it upside down, gently pat it, and unceremoniously drop my smuggled frog onto the bed. The worst punishment my parents inflicted upon me was imprisonment in the house. I couldn't bear not being out in nature with my animals.

As part of a school project in the fifth grade, my sister Diane was required to write her autobiography. What part did her siblings play in her life, how have they affected her, what do they aspire to be? She diligently recorded our answers in her paper after interviewing each of us in turn. When she asked me, age 4, what I wanted to be when I grew up, I confidently exclaimed: "Lassie!"

Our family was blessed to live in Feeding Hills, Massachusetts, a very small farming town at the time. We lived across the street from Rising's Field, a picturesque hayfield that contained acres and acres of gorgeous, tall grass that kept all of the neighborhood kids occupied for hours. Hiding in the middle of the field and flattening the grass to make "rooms," we surrounded large, dried, blackened mushrooms, our natural smoke bombs, and stomped them to create faux bonfires. The smell of the sweet grass being cut and turned for hay, the beauty and peace of meadow sounds, the exciting feel of cool dusk coming after a lazy, hot summer's day… how lucky we were to grow up in this beautiful area.

Beyond Rising's Field was a vegetable farm, beyond that another hay field and woods, and beyond that the historic Bowles Airport, all filled with miles of trails that equaled hours of happiness for neighborhood kids. Bowles Airport, opened in 1931, was adjacent to a horseracing track that hosted the likes of Seabiscuit. At the time I grew up, it was an airport for small private planes and a favorite riding spot for kids with horses and motorcycles. A nice cut-out in the fence provided a convenient secret opening.

A well-worn dirt path led one through the two fields, the vegetable farm, woods, and through this fence into hours of bliss. There was nothing better than watching the planes all afternoon as they took off and landed, the droning sound so reminiscent of lazy, blue-skies-scattered-with-fluffy-white-clouds spring and summer days. I remember when the airport caught fire one evening when I was in my early teens, the windborne ashes lazily reaching our house and fluttering silently around us as we stood in the gathering dusk, facing the airport in shocked silence and able to see the glowing pulse of flames. It was never rebuilt, but remained abandoned until an industrial park took its place.

I sometimes drive by these places and so fondly remember the good times we kids used to have. We were gone all day, parents never worrying at that time as long as we were home before dark, such a different age. We were free to be kids, roving the neighborhood, little gangs out for clean fun. It was in this setting that I was lucky enough to have grown. It was in this setting that animals became a part of my life and a part of everything I did and was.

CHAPTER 3

When I was four, abiding by my orders, my whole family packed into our nine-seater Buick station wagon and went to pick out a collie puppy. We were excited to get our own "Lassie." We took home a beautiful tri-color male, Laddie, who was so gentle and good to us. I don't remember very much about Laddie because I was so young and he lived such a short life with us, but I do remember how sweet he was and how much he loved us. He played on our backyard pond while we skated on its frozen surface, kindly lending support when we clung to his back, precarious on our skates.

Laddie died at age two after being hit by a car. After three days, my sister Diane finally found him by following paw and blood tracks in the snow. He was in the next-door neighbor's shed, so close and hearing us calling, but too hurt to come. A blood clot took his life that night at the vet clinic. When we were told he died, I was heartbroken.

That spring, my mother received a call from a distant neighbor saying that her German Shepherd female had two puppies. She told us that our Laddie had been the father and she asked us to take one. After the devastation of losing Laddie, I was ecstatic to go pick out another baby. I arrived at the house and skipped with excitement into the kitchen, ponytails swinging in rhythmic happiness, where mother and babies were in a towel-swathed corner. One puppy was the color of spun gold while the other was as black as coal. Both looked like a typical Labrador Retriever. While it was doubtful these puppies were the result of a collie father, my mother said we could pick one out. My older sister Lee and I decided on the coal black puppy and named her Pepper. There was no better dog in the world for a child.

I often snuck out of our house at 5:00 am, mindful of my ever-vigilant mother, avoiding every squeak and creak as I made my way down two sets of stairs to the garage. Quietly lifting the garage door up a foot, I rolled under it in order to make a clean break to the outdoors. This is where my animals were. Even then, I was compelled by a need beyond my control to be in their company.

After rounding up Pepper and my all-black cat Kitty, who held a special love reserved only for me, the three of us headed out to the farm across the street. We climbed an old dirt mound and sat to watch the sunrise. I can still smell the fresh, damp earth, the growing vegetables, see the beautiful sight of the farm sprinklers first going off, water shooting through the air like precious jewels reflecting the vibrant colors of the rising sun's glowing rays. One of my arms hugged Pepper next to me while the other cradled Kitty in my lap. How lucky I am for such exquisite memories. Did I realize this then?

By age 6, after shameless begging, I finally had a real horse. Sugar was an awesome black and white pinto, an ex-barrel racer, with spirit and sass befitting my own. Leading Sugar into the fields and airport across the street, I grabbed a handful of mane and vaulted on her back like a Native American. I can still feel the bounce of her stride and her warmth as I sat upon her, smell the earthy sweetness of her coat, see the beautiful curve of her neck, the black and white mane under my hands that flounced in rhythm with her proud walk.

Entering my teen years, I found that my love for collies had not waned. After seeing an advertisement for collie puppies right in our hometown, my parents took me to see them one crisp fall Sunday afternoon. Pulling up to the fence of the breeder's yard, we found two 6-month-old males, both beautiful blue merles. I finally chose Bear, the prettier one with perfect white teeth and a black band running across his back and over his sides as if he were wearing a saddle. Bear was my baby and I loved him with all my heart. When cancer took him at almost 13, it was a very long time before I had another dog in my life.

My younger times with my animals shaped my life. Having such intense love for so many animals, it was inevitable that unforgettable tragedies occurred. One that will forever be remembered was when I excitedly found that Kitty had given birth to a litter of kittens in our garage one morning. When I returned to check on them before going to school, I was met by a horrific scene in which Pepper, trying to stop their crying, had picked them up one by one, her sharp teeth spilling their entrails like little red ribbons. Pepper was depressed the rest of the day for her "sin," lying on the barn deck, heavy head on paws, red blood drying on her black muzzle while my father buried the remains.

Another one of my kittens tried to eat Pepper's food on an early summer evening. After Pepper snapped at her to warn her away, the kitten kept shaking her head in confusion, one eye dangling, hanging by a thread on her cheek, Pepper's tooth catching it just right. I held this kitten in my lap on the barn stairs for the most agonizing 45 minutes I've ever lived, waiting for my father to come take us to the vet, only to have her taken from my white-knuckled grasp never to return. "We'll take care of it," they told my father.

Yet, I have endless memories of utmost beauty as well. There were long walks in the fields and woods, just me and my dogs and cats. There was the pleasure of riding my horse, being gone for most of the day with a lunch packed in the saddle, pretending the two of us were the only ones left alive in the world. Riding deep into the woods, we found a sun-dappled grove where I reached up to pluck the fat, wild grapes and enjoy their bitter sweetness, warmed by the late afternoon sun.

How wonderful for a child's mind and health, being part of the outdoors, appreciating nature in all its glorious forms. How wonderful that my parents allowed us that. My mother was a stay-at-home mother, there to run to when we needed her, carefully monitoring our lives. My father worked three jobs so we could have everything a kid could want: not computers, computer games, or other anti-feeling, anti-emotional things, but real things that taught imagination, love, and life.

These life lessons from childhood brought me, in a seemingly roundabout way, to that day in 1992. All of these experiences: the tragedy, the good; the pain, the happiness; the heartache, the love, prepared me and left me open to learn so many more lessons. They brought me to travel that road to Amesbury and find a little red pit bull waiting for me.

CHAPTER 4

I met Cheryl in 1989 when I was 24. At that time, I was in the middle of pursuing a master's degree in library science and already had a very good job as a librarian in a medium-sized public library. Cheryl, an LPN, was continuing in school to become an RN. I was also in the middle of having a house built. Cheryl and I ended up building the house together and had a commitment ceremony the next winter.

My parents, in all of their unbelievably wise foresight and generosity, had purchased land in Southampton, Massachusetts when I was twelve. They split this land up into lots, gave a lot to each of their children, and kept a lot for themselves. The lot they gave me is where Cheryl and I built our haven, the one for which we are thankful every day of our lives. My family and Cheryl have allowed me to realize every one of my life-long dreams: to have my animals, to have my beautiful, peaceful property, and to have all the people I love surrounding me. How many others are able to say the same?

In 1991, a year after building our house, the mention of a puppy made its first appearance. Cheryl and I already had three cats. All three were able to enjoy a life of being inside or outside cats due to the remote area in which we lived. Taja, "Wolf Kitty," was adopted from the local shelter. At 4, she was the oldest and was a beautiful, medium-furred dark tortoise with the eyes of an owl framed in a black face. At only seven pounds, she made herself sound as if she were a 500-pound lion when she walked on black paws that were very big for her size.

Her attitude proved as big as she imagined herself to be and she acted more like a guard dog than a cat. She once protected Cheryl and me in the barn one late evening when one of our horses was sick. A coy dog had trotted out of the woods and had begun to pace back and forth in front of the barn door, looking in at Cheryl and me from the darkness beyond, not even afraid when I tried to scare it with the barn rake. Then Taja came down from the barn loft, woken from her sleep by all the activity. When she saw the coy dog, she became very angry. She chased it away from the barn and all the way across the property, yowling and screaming, running on three legs and scratching out with the fourth, claws at full extension. Taja was also our ground hunter, wiping out every squirrel, rabbit, mole, mouse and chipmunk in the area. At the same time, she was the cutest and best cuddler and would settle in your lap if you sat even for a second.

How do I even explain Lily, the sweetest soul I've ever known? She was the middle cat, a 14-pound bulls eye tiger with a white bib on her chest, four white paws, and a white-tipped tail, all extremities looking as if they were carefully dipped in white paint. I still remember picking her out with Cheryl and my best friend Terry when she was a few weeks old, traveling into the bowels of Springfield, Massachusetts on a freezing February evening in 1990 to adopt her. She was so small that the white tip on her tail consisted of 2 white hairs. She liked to be our housecat and would only venture outside with the family.

And Monnie was the new long-furred, gray tortoise acquisition. With Monnie, there wasn't a bird that was safe. What a character! When my family built their house and moved in behind us a few years later, Monnie packed her bags and moved out, deciding that she would be their cat. She liked sole attention. She hated being in a household with the two other cats and instigated many a fight. Her name is actually a softened form of "Monster," due to her often mean interactions with the others. We always attributed this anger to her stay at the shelter before we adopted her. She had been placed in a cage with a larger cat that had bullied her, her fur all tufted and sticking out in clumps from the other cat's dried saliva and bite marks. She stared out through the bars at us with an intelligence and knowingness we just couldn't pass up.

All three of our cats were so different, but all three loved and had their own unique relationship with the puppy that we brought home.

CHAPTER 5

When I first broached the subject of getting a puppy, I was surprised that Cheryl was actually accepting of the idea. There were a few very important reasons for my surprise. The first was that we both had very busy lives between schooling, working extra hours, and caring for a new house. And second, the big one, Cheryl was afraid of dogs. However, she knew how much it meant to me to share my life with animals and I think she first agreed only out of the generosity of her heart. It was also a little scary for the two of us, living alone. Our property was in a sparsely-developed, very dark area with 75 acres of woods across the street and the nearest neighbor a 78-year-old lady, Toby, and her equally old Morgan horse, Corky. I think we both looked forward to the company, comfort, and protection of a dog.

Cheryl and I made our lists and discussed the pros and cons of getting a puppy at this point in our lives. In doing this, we found that the pros very much outweighed the cons, especially in matters of the heart. So began a journey that would prove to change our lives forever after.

Once we agreed to a puppy, Cheryl and I were so excited and had so much fun planning. Very new at this in our adult lives, we thought, "What kind of dog should we get?" Would we be better with a rescue or a purebred, an adult or a puppy? Our questions led us to delve into research on different breeds of dogs. We read books and articles, talked to people, and visited breeders of Rottweilers, Boxers, Chows, and Dobermans. After months of research and visits, we still could not decide. We had reached an impasse.

Wishing to clear our thoughts on the subject for a while, Cheryl and I decided to take a relaxing drive one Sunday afternoon. When we drove to the end of our street and slowly rolled to the stop sign, we glanced across the way into the yard beyond. A family was out, enjoying the beautiful weather, and their dog was outside playing with them. A man was throwing a ball to her and she was jumping so high—straight up in the air—to catch it.

Cheryl asked me, "What kind of dog is that, a Rottweiler?" She leaned forward, squinting to get a better look.

I answered, "No, that looks like a pit bull," guessing, since I had never seen a pit bull in person.

Cheryl had never heard of that breed but started to get excited, saying how *perfect* the dog looked. She was medium-sized, athletic, short-haired with a beautiful brindle coat, and seemed to love being out and about with her people. I agreed with Cheryl and began to get excited myself. Tisha, in all the obliviousness of a ball-chasing, fun-loving dog, changed our lives that day. Life can be funny that way, the best things catching you completely unawares.

We started to read all that we could about pit bulls or, as we learned, American Pit Bull Terriers or American Staffordshire Terriers. We loved the fact that they are a medium-sized breed, short-haired, known to be an excellent family dog and great with children, don't drool, and aren't a very vocal breed. We learned that they are more apt to watch strangers silently, the research pointing to the peculiar fact that they seem to have an uncanny knack for sensing the intentions of people, whether harmful or good.

In all of our research, we inevitably ran into the stereotypes and the negative reputation for which "pit bulls" were known. It was the late 1980's into the early 1990's when these negative stereotypes had reached a fever pitch. Horrified by what we read, we delved even deeper until we found the good, positive stories about the pit bull. The stories that told of how the pit bull had been the all-American dog from the 1800's on. They had been historically known as the family dog and the ranch dog. They had been the jack-of-all-trades and can be seen in many vintage photographs, proudly displayed as part of the family, a child's arm usually slung lovingly around the family pit bull's shoulders. They were bred to be extremely friendly and trustworthy, the human-aggressive gene bred out of them for hundreds of years. They rate higher than the Golden Retriever in American Temperament Testing but are abandoned on the streets by the thousands because they are too kind, sensitive, and loving for the abusers that only want their power and strength for evil purposes. They were even nicknamed the "nursemaid's dog" since they were known to be so good with young children that they were babysitters to them. Their love for children is even a specific breed characteristic!

I was more than sickened when I read article after article on the tortures used by abusive people who try to make pit bulls mean attack or protective dogs, which is the complete opposite of their very nature. Methods such as hanging by wire, rubbing gunpowder in wounds, beating, electrocuting, breaking bones, burning, throwing out of high-rise windows, starving, enforcing solitary confinement, and so on... Many times, as they are subjected to a painful death, they still prefer to lick rather than bite the hands that abuse them. I could cry an ocean of tears for these beautiful souls that are tortured for the very qualities that we admired and cultivated in them.

It's just so hard for me to believe that such abusive people exist and are able to do this to other living creatures. Personally, I do not put human beings on a higher scale than animals, so I see these things as an equal offense when done to animals. But, even those people who claim "they're just dogs," "they're just animals," or "they're put here for us to use," have no ground to stand on whatsoever. It is a proven fact that people who can do these things to animals usually "escalate" to abusing or killing other people.

More sickening was the media, sensationalizing all of the negative aspects of pit bulls. It didn't seem to matter that other dogs bite, that everyone I knew, including myself, was bitten by a dog other than a pit bull. My own collie Bear, although I loved him to death, was one of the worst biters I'd ever known. No, you only seemed to hear about pit bulls. Where were all the good stories about these dogs? Where were stories about the pit bulls who were search and rescue dogs, or Stubby, the pit bull war hero, or the pit bulls who were drug and bomb sniffing dogs for the police? The more we read, the more the "pit bull" became an intangible, all-powerful monster of unrealistic proportions. The term became vague, associated with any dog that resembled an American Staffordshire Terrier. This negative attention was more *sensational*, more *newsworthy*, more *exciting*. It just so happens that the sensationalism is at the expense of many innocent souls. How unethical and immoral of these journalists. They made it sound as though the pit bull wasn't flesh and blood anymore, capable of love, pain, and sorrow. Instead, it became a robotic mass of muscle and teeth with no redeeming qualities and could "turn" against anyone at any time. One newspaper article even stated that they were impervious to pain!

What sickened me most were the articles on actual attacks on humans by pit bulls. Having had three pit bulls now and knowing countless others, I cannot even imagine what it takes in order for one to bite a human being. My veterinarian cannot say enough about the temperament of my Aderyn, who licks his face as he's drawing her blood for heartworm testing and who actually *likes* going to the vet since it means meeting people. He's not seen anything like her. I have much empathy for the victims of these attacks and it breaks my heart to think that the experience might cause them and those who know them to denigrate the breed as a whole. I wish I could tell these people that that isn't the real pit bull. I wish I could tell them to please not hold all pit bulls accountable. I wish I could tell them that these dogs are victims, the victims of people at their worst, and we should feel the moral obligation to save them, not to hurt them further by treating them differently from every other dog. I wish I could tell them that the real pit bull has been bred through the centuries to love people and would rather die a thousand painful deaths than bite a person, the most treasured and beloved thing in her/his life.

As one who always tries to be fair in life, I could not believe these injustices. And, especially as an animal lover, I couldn't believe the horror that these fellow creatures, these beautiful souls that *we* created and bred to be most loyal to *us*, had to now endure. All of this research led Cheryl and me down the path to becoming advocates for these dogs, passionate in our loyalty to the cause of saving these misunderstood and misrepresented creatures. Not only was it imperative for us to save these lives as a whole, but the cause became personal as well. Thus, it became our mission to conquer the macrocosm of the injustice in the microcosm of our small world with our little puppy. What a heavy weight she had on her shoulders.

Chapter 6

After picking out our baby and returning from Amesbury, it was such a very difficult wait for Cheryl and me. We spent a lot of time preparing just to try to make the time go by faster. We couldn't stop talking about her and how our new life would be with her. We were just so in love with her already! We shopped and bought leashes, collars, bowls, toys, a crate, and a nice run for the back yard that we set up between two beautiful trees.

But, the weeks were still fraught with worry. Would Wade remember which puppy we chose? He didn't write anything down. He had also told us how people would sometimes try to bribe him with more money for a particular puppy that was already sold. We were especially worried about this with our little baby and her perfect, full-black little muzzle, black-rimmed eyes offset by black-tipped eyebrows, and deep red color. Would this happen to our Chilli Pepper? Would the puppies be okay and stay healthy? On and on went the worries as we waited to pick up our baby.

The call finally came 3 ½ weeks later, two weeks earlier than expected, left on our answering machine for us to hear in our excitement when we got home from work. "Hello, Chilli Peppah is ready to go!" Wade's strong voice said. She was only 5 ½ weeks old but already stomping all over her littermates and eating on her own. She was already the strong and independent soul she was meant to be.

We called Wade right back and made plans to meet with him the weekend of March 15, 1992. It was a sunny, perfect Saturday for our drive to Amesbury, so surprisingly warm without a hint of the bitter winds for which March can be known. It set the most perfect, happy

17

mood. When we reached the yard and pulled in the driveway, we eagerly jumped out at Wade's enthusiastic greeting, seeing people and children in every direction playing with all the dogs. As Wade brought us over to Leigha's puppy pen, the yips and barking paved our way. We could see many of the puppies outside the whelping house playing in the dirt in the warm afternoon sun.

"Is she one of these outside?" we asked Wade excitedly.

"No," he laughed, "she seems to be one of the few in the box, probably eating. I'll get her." In he went and out he came with a fat, roly-poly puppy hanging from his large hand, feet dangling in midair.

"Here she is!" he exclaimed as he handed her to me.

I took her reverently, completely checking her perfect little body in order to make sure that she was the right puppy, checking her full black little muzzle and her black-rimmed eyes, the white on her chest, and the one white toe on her back left foot. Although her color had faded to a delicious vanilla instead of the deep red of that 2 ½-week-old puppy, she was our baby, the one we had picked out! She didn't make a sound as I held her up in the air above me and inspected her so, turning her this way and that. She just gazed down at me steadily, her stare so frank and open and trusting. Cheryl had followed Wade into his house and I jogged to catch up with them, the baby cradled protectively in my arms against my chest.

As we all sat at the kitchen table, I reluctantly put Chilli down so she could sniff curiously around the floor of Wade's kitchen. Wade's wife and 3-year-old daughter, Leigha (after whom I assume Chilli's mother was named), joined us to visit. We finished filling out the paperwork for Chilli and paid Wade the other half of the $300 we owed him for her purchase. As we were doing this, Wade again told us how much he appreciated dealing with us as customers.

"It is always such a relief and a worry off my mind when I see one of my puppies go with good family people," he said. "Sometimes it's so hard letting my puppies go with others."

I could tell that he wanted to make sure that Cheryl and I understood what we were getting with this breed of which he was so proud, so he continued with feeling, "She'll be a good pup for you, this breed is the best. Leigha, as a baby, once crawled up to one of my males who was sleeping on the floor and bit him in the balls. All he did was get up and walk away. I wouldn't have been able to do that! My kids and nieces and nephews are always here playing with my dogs."

When he stopped speaking, Leigha, roughly scooping Chilli up in a clumsy toddler way, asked, "Will she be an inside dog or outside dog?" Chilli hung there uncomfortably, her fat stomach in Leigha's two pudgy hands as Leigha looked expectantly at us for our answer.

Cheryl quickly said "A little bit of both, Honey. Now, can you put the puppy down? She doesn't seem to want to be held." Cheryl was always the direct one, always saying what I wished to be able to say, always looking out for the best for us all.

After everything was finished, we took our puppy and started for home. I was driving Cheryl's white Honda Accord while she held Chilli in her lap swaddled in a towel. The puppy was so small that she fit on Cheryl's lap the long way, in between her legs, with room to spare. Back we headed down that literal and proverbial road to our new life together. How trusting these babies are to go along with complete strangers, to enter a whole new world so bravely, to march to the beat of our drum into a new life and nothing in the world that they know.

CHAPTER 7

Cheryl and I never mentioned anything about our puppy to my family. We pictured such a joyful surprise for when we finally introduced her to everyone. All of those weeks, we held in our news. By the time Chilli was ready, we were bursting to show her off—so proud of this perfect little creature already. My family still lived in the house where I grew up in Feeding Hills, approximately a ½ hour ride from my home in Southampton. That Sunday, the day after we picked her up, we brought Chilli to meet my family.

On our first trip together, this little 6-week old baby slept the whole way, snuggled warmly in a nice soft blanket as we meandered along route 187, winding through Westfield into Feeding Hills. We decided to first stop at my brother, Paul's, and his girlfriend, Katie's, house. With the sleepy puppy wrapped securely, we approached their front door. Paul and Katie answered the knock to the unusual sight of us, since we rarely visited them. Seeing our bundle, they probably wondered with great curiosity what we brought to show them. We all made our way to the bedroom that they shared where we unwrapped the blanket, unveiling a fat speck. Paul and Katie leaned in for a look, so excited to see a puppy. They asked her name and we said we had not yet come up with one, but that her registered name was Chilli Pepper. Little did we know that we would debate over names for 9 more weeks before finding the right one, calling her "Baby" and numerous other nicknames in the meantime.

After we all talked and played with Chilli for a while, Cheryl and I decided to press on. We left Paul and Katie and their enthusiastic well wishes to drive the two miles to my parents' house. We pulled down

20

their driveway and parked. Darkness had arrived and we climbed the back stairway to the deck, feeling our way up as we approached the door. My older brother Rob answered our knock and quickly flipped on the lights. As he opened the door, he saw that I was carrying something in a blanket.

"What do you have?" he asked curiously.

I opened the blanket to reveal our little puppy. He leaned in to say, "Oh, how cute –"

At the same time I said, "She's a pit bull." This caused Rob to stop mid-sentence and jump backward saying, "No!... Really?" Oh, how his reaction would change in the future, how *she* would change it.

As we introduced Chilli to my family—my mother, my father, Rob, my oldest sister, Diane, and my next older sister, Lee—Chilli was friskily and busily running around the kitchen, excitedly checking all nooks and crannies, scoffing up any crumbs or goodies she could find. She finally tired, dropped in the middle of the floor, and promptly fell asleep. We all sat on the kitchen floor surrounding her, talking quietly as she soundly slept. My family had heard so much negative publicity about this breed and had never met one in person, so they asked Cheryl and me numerous questions. Why did we choose her? Did we do our research? Would she be a good family dog? As the years went by, my whole family became experts on pit bulls. They, as much as I, developed a deep, all-consuming love for them and proudly explained to people the truth about this beautiful breed. Little did we know how pit bulls would become a passion for all of us, and we would be fighting for their very lives in the distant future. But for now, questions and answers were discussed well into the evening, and my family immediately grew to love this little baby, grunting and snoring in her sleep like a piglet.

That great weight she was born carrying, always having to prove herself just for being a pit bull, was shouldered with the perfect ease of the oblivious. She rose to the occasion by proving that society's imposed prejudice was without merit, her strength and beauty evident from the very beginning, so strong in body and spirit. She was our rock, each of us using her as that bottomless reservoir of strength from which to draw when needed. Because she was pure in her giving, complete in her innocence, we received everything we needed from her, whether it was sympathy, a shoulder to cry on, a warm body to hug and kiss, or just love and licks to be given when we might be feeling down.

Cheryl and I loved our lives so much with the new puppy right from the start. She brought us so much fun, so much laughter, so much love. Soon after, I realized she did the same for my whole family.

CHAPTER 8

Cheryl and I both have ultra-responsible personalities and tend to research everything to an obsessive degree in order to make informed decisions. When we were doing our research on raising a puppy, we found that "crating" was becoming *the* thing to do. I have to admit, I wasn't too thrilled about crating a dog and didn't like the idea of caging her. I told Cheryl, though, "I'll keep an open mind about this crating thing. But, we have to make the crate as homey as possible for our baby. And, it's only going to be used for when we aren't home. I want her to sleep with us."

Cheryl agreed. Our bedroom is our haven, emitting an aura of complete peace, love, and relaxation. Each night, after our busy day, we all made our way upstairs together, Lily always joining us. Cheryl or I picked Chilli up and placed her on the bed where she immediately collapsed, stretched out on her side, and fell into the deepest sleep. She found the perfect and, of course, best spot: in between us. At first, her size worried us so much. Both of us were afraid that, in our sleep, we might crush such a small creature.

Another worry that came with sleeping with her was her potty schedule. The two of us agreed to take turns bringing her out at night, carrying her down the stairs from the second-floor bedroom, out the front door, and placing her on the grass in the front yard.

Sometimes, Chilli didn't even piddle when I brought her out on these late night excursions. She groggily collapsed where I placed her, her head bobbling as she fell asleep where she sat. I stood there in the cold, the spring peepers not even out yet, shivering and willing Chilli to potty quickly as I watched her and waited. When it looked as though

23

nothing was going to happen, I picked her up to trudge back up the stairs once again, where she fell back to sleep immediately.

That first week we had Chilli, we thought that she was such a good puppy, able to sleep through the night and hold her bladder so long already. We hadn't ever had a puppy with which we slept, so Cheryl and I didn't realize that something wasn't quite right about this. Every morning, we woke up and commented on how good she was, smiling and looking at each other so proudly, saying, "What a good, easy puppy, sleeping through the night!"

But, at the end of the week, I found out how wrong we were. When I started to change the sheets, I noticed little pee spots all over the bed. What a funny little baby—she just wasn't going to ruin a good night's sleep!

CHAPTER 9

The new puppy loved and fit in with her sisters immediately, each cat interacting with her so differently. Taja absolutely loved dogs. When Cheryl and I had lived in an apartment in Holyoke before building our house, our roommates had dogs. Taja loved to curl up with them to sleep, but loved to tease them just as much. One of the dogs, Anchor, tried in vain to get onto the pantry counter where he knew his biscuits were kept. If the mood struck her, Taja went into the pantry, jumped on the counter, and knocked the box over for him. This caused a cascade of biscuits to be spilled within Anchor's reach. This wasn't completely altruistic on Taja's part; she was just so smart that she knew Anchor always left crumbs that she got to enjoy herself. Taja loved this new baby that Cheryl and I brought home. She was never jealous, rather she loved all the added fun and activity that Chilli brought into our lives.

Lily, always the shy one, hovered in the background, quietly watching and studying this new little terror, peeking out from under the stairway or from behind the couch or chair. I'm sure she mostly wondered how all of this would affect her favorite sleeping spots. When she was the last cat left to us, she and this baby became the best of buddies, developing such a deep love for each other and a bond that I've never seen stronger between two animals. Lily appreciated the protection and love that Chilli gave to her and Chilli recognized the sweet, gentle soul that Lily was and respected her completely.

Monnie was a different story. From the very start, she never liked sharing her life with other animals. The new puppy put her in a very foul mood indeed and pushed her over the edge on which she had been hovering. Seeming to know this, Chilli teased Monnie most of all, continuing this harassment well into both their old age. Ass in the air, front paws down in a playful pose, Chilli loved to corner Monnie, barking at her with a bratty puppy yelp, black muzzle acrinkle. Turning her head this way and that, looking for something nearby to shred, she already perfected that sassy sideways look that became her trademark, dodging the claws coming at her, as quick and deadly as lightning. Monnie's grey ears flattened sideways to her head in complete anger and irritation. The baby never saw the danger in this, only the fun in the torment. Eventually intervening, Cheryl or I picked up the wriggling, struggling puppy to remove her from Monnie's murderous intentions.

With three cats as her sisters, Chilli watched and imitated them, thinking for the longest time that she was a cat, too. She crawled up our couch and walked along its narrow back, found a nice sunny spot on top and curled up to sleep, snuggling in a tight ball on the cushions as if she was one of her sisters. She continued to do this for a few years until she decided she was too good for things like that. After all, I truly believe she came to think of herself as one of us: not a cat, and definitely not a dog.

CHAPTER 10

On one of our first nights with Chilli, I wearily got up in the predawn cold to take her out to potty. Bundling myself in sweats, I picked up her sleeping body, carried her down the stairs and out the front door. I stood sleepily, blowing great plumes of frosted air into the chilly morning. The naked trees' branches were stark, reaching toward the colorful hint of a beautiful pink and powder blue sunrise. Chilli just sat there, eventually falling over, sound asleep.

Shaking my head, I picked her up and carried her into our cozy, warm house, back upstairs, and placed her on the bed. I turned away for one second to take off my sweatpants, then turned back to the bed to see...no Chilli! There was just a slight indentation in the comforter where a puppy had been! Then, a dawning realization of horror as my gaze wandered downward, not wanting to acknowledge what I knew I'd see. Probably waddling over to the edge of the bed, trying to see what I was doing, Chilli had fallen while my back was turned. It might as well have been a cliff to this six-week old baby who was now on the floor, struggling to stand, one perfect front paw twisted at an awful angle. She looked up at me in surprise, not making a sound, wondering why she couldn't put her right front leg down.

I woke Cheryl in a panic, telling her what happened and peppering her with questions. "Should we get her to the vet? What if she broke her leg and needs a cast? I can't believe this just happened—what is wrong with me?"

Cheryl told me to calm down as she looked Chilli over, gently holding her paw and examining the injury. As she was manipulating

Chilli's joint, she said, "No, just come back to bed and let's go to sleep. She's in no distress so let's see what happens when we wake up."

Even in the midst of Cheryl's calm assurances, I felt like such a negligent mother. How could I have not watched her, how could I have let this baby we received in the most perfect condition become marred in any way? How could I have been so irresponsible to the one that trusted me so unconditionally? I berated myself.

I finally took Cheryl's advice with great hope that everything would be okay, but, at the same time, I knew that I would never be able to forgive myself if my baby was terribly hurt due to my stupidity. So, with this responsibility weighing heavily on my restless mind, I scooped up my puppy and protectively cuddled her warm, trusting body. I placed her against my beating heart and whispered in her little ear how sorry I was as we drifted off to sleep.

A few hours later we all woke up to a bright, sunny morning, the dark situation of a few hours ago like a bad dream. I quickly looked at Chilli as she woke, standing to gaze back at me, wondering at my instant worry. To my great relief, I found her standing and walking normally on all legs. In her sleep and probably due to her youth, her paw must have adjusted itself back! Oh, the relief I felt, such weight off my heart! I picked her up and hugged her tightly. Right then and there, I vowed to *never* take my eyes or hands off her like that ever again.

My little roly poly puppy, so fat and healthy, beautiful puppy with the mascara eyes, I love you so much it hurts.

CHAPTER 11

Cheryl and I were so excited to try out all the new things that we had purchased for our puppy. One of the first things we tried was her run in the back yard that Cheryl and I so painstakingly made sure was perfect, in between two beautiful, shady trees. We didn't even give it a second thought, not realizing that anything could go amiss. We confidently carried her outside on the first warm day, all pretty in her new collar, and brought her to the run.

I placed Chilli down in the grass as Cheryl unhooked the clasp from the line, clipping it to the puppy's little collar. At first, Chilli didn't notice, falling over sideways as she dipped down to chew on some new spring sprigs of green grass. While upside down, her little puppy needle teeth chewed on the run wire for a while, paws waving wildly in fun. Cheryl and I smiled, both of us so calm, oblivious to the fact that we were in the eye of a storm. When Chilli struggled to right herself, she realized that something was... different.

After a few seconds, as comprehension slowly dawned on this evolving manipulator, the storm broke loose and sheer panic ensued. Chilli screamed and howled and fought the line, backing up on her hindquarters and biting at the cable while clawing it with both front paws. For one so small, she certainly fought like a tiger and sounded even worse, a horribly loud racket of screeching and yelping coming out of her that reached decibels previously unheard of. It was so horrible that we finally rescued her, worried that she might break her neck in her frantic fight, and also worried that our neighbors might think that a puppy was getting murdered in our yard.

We ran back to her, picked up her struggling, straining body, and unclipped the line. We stared at each other as we put her down, mortified, breathing hard with worry. As if nothing had happened, the baby frolicked happily among the grass, sticks, and leaves in the back yard—free at last.

We were shocked at such a strong reaction. Of course, she hadn't been on a leash yet (and rarely would be thereafter), but this puppy tantrum had been severe. So, Cheryl and I quickly talked it over while we watched the now cute, good little puppy, wondering what had gone so wrong. We agreed to swallow our fear and sympathy and try again. This time we would leave her, not go to her rescue, so that she could work out her tantrum. As a trainer would say, "Teach her how it's going to be, and that's that."

After all was said and done, it was Cheryl and I who were taught "how it was going to be." No matter what we did, Chilli always got free—every time without fail. Cheryl and I left Chilli and went in the house, occasionally looking out the back bay window to check the puppy's progress. All we saw was a very happy puppy, once again frolicking around loose, the run line swinging in the wind with an empty little collar at its end. After those initial attempts and failures, Chilli's beautiful and lovingly thought-out run was abandoned to the elements. It first became a wonderful clothesline, and later, a great suet hanger for the birds.

The second lesson Cheryl and I learned had to do with Chilli's crating. When Cheryl and I prepared her crate, we took such loving care in making it as nice as could be. I already held guilt about putting her in a crate, so we went the extra mile and stuffed it with items that would comfort and occupy a puppy. Before Cheryl and I left for work, we placed Chilli in her crate. Turning, she looked at us through the bars, so cute, black eyebrows arched, questioning what was next and staring at us with intensity beyond her age. "You're *really* not leaving me in this thing, are you?"

Once she realized that, yes, that *was* the plan, the howling commenced. Throwing her head back, her little black-rimmed mouth forming a circle, she howled as loud and as mournful as any wolf cub. Occasionally, she stopped and gave us her infamous sideways look, allowing us another chance to change our minds. Then the howling started all over again when she didn't get her way. We walked away as she bit and tore at the metal in a frenzy, howling, knowing even at her young age that people, unless punished, aren't caged. She attacked the metal door, little paws clawing and pushing in terror. Her fight with the crate was so terrible that we had to wire the door shut so it wouldn't open in her struggles.

It broke our hearts to do this, and we had to steel our emotions in order to leave her. But, we thought we had to, and we were assured that dogs grow to *love* their crates. So, we stuck with it, thinking that she would outgrow her hate. It only got worse. My family even found excuses not to babysit anymore, unable to bring themselves to put her back in her crate when they left. Even my father, who came to work on the property almost daily and let her out to enjoy the yard while he worked, didn't let her out any more. He told us, "I just can't stand putting her back in there."

Cheryl and I realized that something was wrong if all of us were feeling the same way. We considered the possibility of abandoning Chilli's confinement. After another talk similar to the run discussion, we made the decision to try allowing Chilli her freedom. Then, we waited to see what would happen.

Chilli's adjustment to this freedom went surprisingly well except for two destructive "accidents" and a third "accident" that wasn't as destructive as it was funny. Unfortunately, one of the destructive accidents left me without something that I had treasured since childhood, something that was very important to me. This important, well-loved item was my stuffed lamb that I received for Easter when I was 4. When I was in my teens, my grandmother lovingly restored her tattered body after the many years I had spent hugging her. This lamb was one of my most cherished possessions and I made sure to keep her up on a windowsill, well out of reach of a mischievous puppy. Despite my precautions, Cheryl came home from work one day, horrified to find pieces of Lambie strewn all over the house. I remember Cheryl's hesitant call to me at work that day, so afraid to tell me. I was very upset, but quickly calmed down, thinking that everything would be okay. Once home, I'd collect Lambie's pieces, and have her restored, once again.

Once I returned home and witnessed the carnage for myself, I found out how naïve this plan had been. Not only was Lambie torn apart, but many pieces were missing. The pieces that were left were unrecognizable, except for one small piece of her face that consisted of one of her sweet, sleeping eyes, her cute pink nose, and the pink flower in her hair. I kept this piece with me for a long time until, sadly, I accepted the fact that Lambie would never be resurrected.

The second situation involved a pillow. Again, it was Cheryl who came home from work to the puppy's masterpiece. She walked in the front door and looked up to see that our loft room was covered in inches of feathers, from one end to the other, smaller feathers lazily floating down and around to the living room floor. Chilli had taken one of our bedroom pillows, dragged it into our loft room, and proceeded to tear it apart, slapping it to the ground and side-to-side as if she were throttling a snake. I would have never guessed that a pillow contained so many feathers. The puppy greeted Cheryl at the door laughing and panting, more feathers stuck to her tongue. She was so very happy and so very proud of such complete and thorough work.

The third situation involved another cherished item of mine, desecrated but not really destroyed: the Raggedy Ann doll that my aunt made for me. Instead of true carnage, Raggedy Ann was just undressed—her knickers found in one room, her apron in another, her dress, all wet and balled up with saliva, left on the living room floor. Raggedy herself, in all her naked glory, had been abandoned in the bedroom, maybe stripped but, thankfully, whole.

Did you know this, my funny little girl? Did you know that these items mattered to me, so took it upon yourself to "put them in their place," below you, making it your quest to be #1 in my life? You needn't have worried, as you must have come to know, as I should have told you right away... right from the beginning, you were my one and only true love...

After these few incidents, the puppy was an angel. She never touched anything again and we were confident that we could leave anything out in the house: shoes, slippers, papers on the table or on the stairway. Even at Christmastime, she never touched a present, not even ones obviously wrapped for her, some of them with smells I can't imagine how she resisted. They were under the tree for weeks until Christmas day, when she knew it was finally time to help us open our gifts, and open her own presents herself.

CHAPTER 12

"What's in a name?" Shakespeare's Juliet muses, opining that a name doesn't necessarily hold the qualities or inherent properties of the named.

Although I agree, at the same time, I loved this new little life so much that the name Cheryl and I chose for her had to be ideal. She had already brought so much to our lives and we wanted to acknowledge her importance, the irreplaceable niche she had already carved out. I was so sure she was destined for great things, a special purpose. We didn't want to pick a name hastily but wanted to pick one out with great and loving care that would fit her properly.

For those reasons, it took us 9 weeks. Cheryl and I perused our lists upon lists of names, only creating more problems for all the choices we gave ourselves. We sat in bed at night for hours, lights dim, quietly discussing the names we each liked while the puppy slept, the TV on low. I stopped to stare at her tiny body and pointed out to Cheryl something she might be doing in her sleep to make us both softly laugh. There, she was lying snoring, completely content after a day full of fun and play, so beautiful and pudgy, belly so big and round, small legs stretched out stiffly. She suckled in her sleep, searching in vain for a mother's milk that wasn't there. We watched her and wondered, "What would fit such a perfect, joyous little soul?"

What would be the best name for this little puppy with the funniest, most clownish personality, but still a puppy so knowing, intelligent, and wise from the very beginning? I thought back to that first day in Wade's yard as I held her above me against the sun, her body haloed, staring into eyes that knew the meaning of life.

Then, it finally came. Not even a name that had made our list, but a name I saw one day, stamped so beautifully into the cover of an old book while passing by a shelf in the library. After it was said, there was no other: Rumer. Rumer, the most perfect name, the most beautiful strong, yet feminine, name. Our little puppy was named after the famous author Rumer Godden, of course.

CHAPTER 13

In 1992, Cheryl and I had slightly different work schedules. Cheryl's hours were earlier than mine, which meant I had Rumer all to myself in the mornings! I loved spending time with Cheryl and Rumer together, of course, but I so loved this special time I had with Rumer, just she and I. I was always so excited to get up very early to prepare her for her day. I woke up thinking, "What will Rumer learn today? What new experiences will Rumer have? How will she make me laugh today?" I felt my love for this little creature grow and grow until it knew no bounds.

Every morning after a quick breakfast, she and I started outside for our walk, beginning a wonderful routine that lasted many years. We are so lucky to have our beautiful property. Rumer and I followed the perimeter, relaxing and enjoying the nature around us. The air was still cold and crisp and sometimes we stepped out onto a fine layer of ice that covered the hopeful grass, her little heated pads melting footprints next to mine, always side by side, hers eventually veering off from mine as she got brave enough to investigate something along the way.

I never brought a leash. Rumer learned her property borders very well and learned to stick by me, although, to be honest, she never wanted to stray far. The only thing she ever chased was a deer once that startled her in the yard and, occasionally, a neighborhood dog that wandered onto her property. Otherwise, she was just happy to watch everything, to smell all the smells, to fling leaves about in the air and chase them in fun when the wind took them away.

Stepping out into the milky almost-spring mornings, the sun's rays weakly pulsing through clouds thick with moisture, we started at the front right corner of our property and took a left at the property line. This line separated our yard from Toby's where Corky, the old Morgan horse, grazed. We followed this line, Toby's beautiful hay field to our right, our property spread out to our left, the leaves blowing gently and peacefully around us, the smell of our pines as sweet as baking bread. The hay field was sometimes covered in a thick mist emanating from the warming earth, with its two ancient apple trees reaching out, ghostly and haunting, in a scene that would be the envy of Avalon.

The hawk pair that nested here answered each other's loudly-screeched questions as we proceeded up the slight slope, toward the back, where the thickness of the woods proved an impenetrable barrier. I was extra protective of Rumer at this stage when she was so little, worried her small body might become a hawk's meal.

Taking another left, we walked along the woods, an area of magnificent treasures for a dog's senses. Covered with leaves, rolling with acorns, peppered with prints and scat of the woodland creatures, it was a dog's paradise. As Rumer scruffed around, digging and snorting, running and playing, I tried to take everything in: her energetic perfection, the peaceful woods to our right, the mist gently floating off the drying trees in the warming early morning sun. I looked down toward my house, the road, and our beautiful rolling hills along with the property's two ponds and three brooks, knowing a brilliant display of yellow buttercups and dandelions would soon appear in the spring fields. On our evening walks, our senses were in heaven. Toby's hay field and our meadow were alight with fireflies, zipping over the sweet-smelling, tall grass, and the peepers in the ponds and brooks were deafening in their happiness that dusk was finally upon them. We took it in, Rumer and I, with great big breaths. We smelled March in Massachusetts, warming mud, the thawing earth, the wind whispering to us through the pines, portents of the spring to come.

One morning as we ambled along, Rumer carrying a freshly dug-up stick, we came upon a flock of starlings. We startled them as we came, a smoky black flock so huge that it actually took shape as it burst up and around us, flying toward the woods in synchronicity. I stared in wonder as it formed the shape of a black bear, then a stag, and then a storm cloud, swollen with thunder! And suddenly, they were gone, dispersed among the trees and lost in shadows.

Mouth open at such a beautiful sight, I looked down at Rumer.

If I had had any doubts before at how special she was, how knowing, they were now completely gone. She was so intuitive it was almost scary. It hit me then, as I looked down at her. I came to the realization that Rumer would prove to be more like my little girl and fulfill any motherly urge I would ever have. She looked back at me with the stick in her mouth like a cigar, eyebrows raised and peppered with droplets of fresh dew. As startled as the starlings, her eyes reflected wonder and awe as much as mine. She seemed to ask, "Was that for real?!" This is how we shared our first moment, the moment that bonded us closer than two souls could ever hope to be.

Rumer and I continued our walk, rounding the back corner of the property. We walked down toward the road, following the opposite property line. This area contained a steep beach-sand hill that quickly became our favorite place. Looking at each other, we took off running, racing each other to the deep sand, hitting the top of the sand dune at full speed and beginning our run down. I laughed so hard as Rumer's little legs tried to keep up with her body as we flew down, sinking deeply. Approaching the bottom, we jumped across the small brook, and crossed the field beyond. Finally, slowing back to a walk, we finished by following the frontage, another line of woods separating us from the road. We followed this line back and approached our house, once again.

It was so cute, at first, on our walks. Rumer was so little, but tried so hard to keep up with me, her short legs and pudgy body clumsily running as she tried to experience everything at once. I pointed things out to her like fresh deer tracks or coy dog prints as she excitedly stuck her nose right into them, getting as much smell as she could. I clapped my hands for her to come back to me if she moved too far away and she came tottering, newfound leaf or stick in her mouth, or sometimes, some stinky and gross unmentionable. Her love for these unmentionables made me scream when she brought them to me, like a gift, chewing and swallowing them quickly when she realized her idea of treasure wasn't necessarily mine. I dove at her to try to stop her, prying open her mouth, shaking it up and down to get the item out, hoping to impress upon her how unwanted this particular behavior was. These unmentionables were just too good, though, and she continued to love these nasty things right to the end.

As a baby, when I called her she came, looking at me with an inquiring expression, so happy with all these treasures she found. Her black eyebrows lifted as she looked me in the eyes to see what I wanted, always looking me right in the eyes. I told her, "Come this way, Rumer. Let's keep going." And, she did. Quickly tiring from trying to fit so much in, I ended up carrying her most of the way.

I loved these walks every morning with Rumer. This puppy was a complete and utter joy. She found pleasure in the most inane things. I watched her run and frisk about, thinking how much she reminded me of a little horse. Her body, though tiny, was so perfect in every way, muscular, solid, and conformed just right. Pudgy, yet square, she stood like a Quarter Horse, all power and muscle sitting atop paws so big for her size. I picked her up, not able to keep my hands off of her perfection, held her dangling in front of me, and just looked at her while she still let me. And, she did let me faun over her and kiss her tiny black mush. Becoming quickly impatient, she wiggled in that puppy way to be let down for more sniffs and fun. "So much to do, so little time," she seemed to say, a foreshadowing of my life with her.

The desire to remember everything about her so important to me, I often try to think of Rumer's eyes as a baby, to remember their color as I held her up and inspected her so closely, so lovingly. I cannot remember for the life of me if they started out blue and became her lovely chocolate brown. Did they change as Aderyn's eyes did, starting out blue and running a gamut of colors, from hazel to green to her present golden yellow, as stunning as a lioness? I can't remember and this annoys me. When I finally ask Lee in my frustration, she tells me with complete surety that Rumer's eyes were always her beautiful chocolate brown.

Chapter 14

Every Sunday and holiday, Cheryl and I visited my parents' house for family fun and good food. Of course, this now included Rumer. To not have her was unheard of.

After our half-hour drive, the three of us pulled in my parents' driveway. Rumer always seemed to sense our last turn and woke up (she was such a good traveler) from her dozing, excitedly sitting up between Cheryl and me on the bench seat in my pickup, shaking and whining with excitement. We pulled down the steeply sloping drive and opened the truck door. Out Rumer flew, running as fast as she could up the back stairs to the back door, a yellow streak with leash trailing behind in her wake. The door magically opened and she entered to a welcome Cheryl and I didn't even get, hugs and kisses and screaming, as she ran around the house exuberantly greeting everyone. She was always the center of attention and began to accept it this way only. And, we never really thought any differently. Whatever we did, Rumer was always a part of it.

As we were driving to my parents' one week during that summer of Rumer's puppyhood, a police car edged in behind me and, with a "whoop whoop", pulled me over to the side of the road. Rumer loved to "drive," knowing that this was the place of importance, and would *not* settle for sitting anywhere else than on the driver's lap. Cheryl and I had purchased a Toyota 4Runner when we decided to get Rumer with great plans of traveling with her in this nice big vehicle, making the whole back area hers by putting the seats down and spreading blankets, a dog's dream. But, no, we found out quickly that she would not have that.

So, there we sat, the three of us all squished up front, Rumer typically "driving" while the cavernous back was empty.

I carefully pulled over, police lights flashing in my rearview mirror, and quickly pushed Rumer over to the passenger side onto Cheryl's lap. The police officer approached slowly and bent down to squint in the car at all of us. A finger pulled his sunglasses below his eyes as he stared at me hard. After a long glare, he said dryly, "You know your dog can't sit there, right?"

As I assessed his mood, I quickly realized that he really wouldn't like any excuses or explanations such as, "Well, Rumer really likes to drive." Or, "We can't tell Rumer that she can't sit at the wheel, she gets upset." So, instead, I apologized profusely.

After more dirty looks and not a hint of a smile, he "let us off" with a warning. Thanks to this close call, we had to get more firm with Rumer than we ever had to before. We explained to her that, although she thought she was still that small baby that could fit anywhere, she couldn't drive anymore. From then on, she had to be content with sitting in the passenger seat. She was not happy with us at all.

CHAPTER 15

I come from a large Italian family where homemade, delicious food has always been plentiful. My mother's mother emigrated from Italy, bringing with her a knack for making better food than any gourmet chef. The smell of her house, of garlic and roasted peppers and a hint of sweet bread, was the best smell in the world. They say our sense of smell is the most potent, with just a slight waft of something able to bring age-old memories sharply to the surface. This is so true for me with my grandmother, Ma. A whiff of dough, of garlic and pepper, of sauce mingled with cheese, will bring memories of me as a child helping her to make our pizzas, she generously missing the pan as she sprinkled on the cheese since I was allowed to eat anything that fell on the counter.

Not only was her food the best, but she passed on this joy and talent for cooking to all her daughters as well. My mother was no exception. From desserts to meals, she has no equal, and homemade food is always available. Because of this, our house was always chaotic with company, from neighborhood kids to family and friends. There was always fun to be had and parties galore.

We had holiday parties, Easter egg-coloring contests, anniversaries… Rumer was always there, a part of the festivities, treated as a granddaughter and niece. Her feet almost never touched the ground when she was a baby because one of us always wanted to hold her. What became my mother's greatest joy was to carry "her" little baby around like a human in the crook of her arm, Rumer resting on her hip. Rumer hung there, paws dangling outward, looking around from this great perspective with an excellent view of all the food and goodies on our dining room table. Grammie held her like this as she was cooking, sitting at the table talking, eating, or just walking around, and Rumer was content to be in the center of all the activity. She never had a need for anything, all needs being met before she even knew of them.

My father's favorite activity with Rumer was to get on the kitchen floor, on his hands and knees, and go at her with his head down, his hands defending himself, pushing her six-pound body backwards on the slippery floor. She struggled gamely to get through his defenses, toddling, baby growling and yipping, front paws pushing on hands bigger than she. Eventually, with her baby needle teeth and cat-like claws, she found Papa's head at which point he got up laughing and exclaiming, "That puppy!"

As she got older and more rambunctious, Rumer loved to run into my parents' bedroom, a room off limits to anyone else. I believe she knew this and flaunted her privilege to the rest of us. She took her time in there and sniffed around curiously, mischievously seeking anything to steal in order to add to the fun and make everyone laugh. She thought she hit the jackpot if my mother left her nylons anywhere within her reach. She came bucking and rearing out of my parents' room, flipping the nylons in the air, and took a sharp left into the living room. There, the shredding commenced, making my mother laugh and laugh despite the destruction of her expensive nylons because *Rumer* was having fun. Rumer always did everything with such a sense of humor and joy that, no matter what, it was *funny,* and you just couldn't get mad at this little joker.

On one visit, a cousin of mine stopped over for dinner. She brought her son Billy, who was 5 years old. He loved playing with Rumer and tired her out until she finally collapsed in her favorite sleeping place, her beanbag chair next to the dining room table. She slept soundly here no matter how loud the talking and laughing. Billy conveyed a story to all of us about their family pit bull since they had one, too. He said, "My pit bull can climb fences (or, as he said it "fenthis). It struck me as funny then how people with pit bulls always seemed to talk about them the same way. They never said the usual "my dog" or "Buffy." Instead, they said "My Pit Bull." It was always a statement made with such pride.

I could understand this, for I was now one of the proud ones.

Chapter 16

When Rumer was a puppy in the early 1990's, I was just finishing up my Master's of Library Science degree. I was attending Southern Connecticut State University and, since there were no online courses at that time, had to drive almost 2 hours each way to attend classes. In order to accomplish this, I took one day off during the week for school and worked every Saturday to make up for that day. It was a hard few years, but worth it.

That first year of Rumer's life, I attended classes on Thursdays. Conveniently, that was the day my sister Lee had off from work. She loved Rumer so much from the very start and once told me that she loved Rumer more than she ever thought was possible to love anything, as though she had given birth to Rumer herself. The depth of their love for each other was quite astounding.

Cheryl and I so appreciated Lee's feelings. We never had to worry about a babysitter when one was needed. On my way to school, I brought Rumer, her food ready and mixed in a container, some toys, and any last minute instructions to Lee, leaving her in Lee's capable hands all day. During Rumer's very rebellious stage, I sometimes literally dropped her off and peeled out, like a typical mother fed up with a morning of resistance and brattiness. Lee stood there with an armful of wriggling, rebelling puppy, food containers, and toys, watching my dust as I took off, her parting words lost in the squeal of tires.

These early character-forming times with Lee were some of the most important and educational moments in Rumer's life. Lee is the one who spent hours with Rumer, solely and completely. They filled the whole day with each other's company. She helped to mold and shape Rumer into the beautiful little soul she became.

One of the things Lee taught Rumer was the meaning of words and phrases. Beginning with the word "smell," Lee told her, "Come on, Rumer, let's go investigate," and together they traversed my parents' yard. Lee stopped occasionally to point out flowers, something half-buried, or a hole some creature scratched out the night before and say, "Rumer, come here, smell this." Rumer did, pudgy little body running this way and that, tottering over to see or sniff the new and exciting things Lee showed her. She did anything for her Auntie Lee. After a while, all any of us needed to say was, "Rumer, smell," and she did, pressing her nose to a paw print here or clump of mud there.

Lee also made much use of her camcorder on these days and was responsible for all the videos we have of Rumer. Lee used to joke that Rumer probably thought the camcorder was a part of her face, she took so many videos. Because of Lee's diligence, we saw what made up their day. We watched how Rumer tired after playing, falling asleep in her beanbag chair, her neck hanging over her favorite toys Clyde and Dale, my horse slippers. We watched her clumsily chase after a leave blowing in the wind in the back yard or a stick Lee threw for her. Sometimes Rumer flipped something in the air and it landed unseen behind her so her head flicked back and forth to find it, she not being able to follow its path since her puppy coordination wasn't quite able to yet. We saw her chase Rob, my older brother, around the back yard, up and down their steep hill. Rumer ran so hard trying to catch him, huffing and puffing in her frustration and anger as she passed us on her chase, eyes intently on Rob, her short legs and small body not yet cooperating with what her mind wanted. And, this is where we can go back to just remember her, how she looked, the way her cute, throaty little bark sounded as she threw back her head and yelled at Lee for any discipline attempted toward her.

Cheryl and I worried so much about Rumer during the time when she was a baby. She didn't know when to give up or to rest, and played until she dropped, not wanting to miss anything. You had to actually tell her when to stop and put her down for a nap like a child. Just because she wouldn't stop playing didn't mean she had an endless amount of energy, she just didn't want to disappoint. This breed wants to please their humans so much that they will die to do so. We worried that my family wouldn't remember this. Lee, who is ultra-responsible and "motherly," was entrusted with our little baby. Lee loved to settle Rumer in her beanbag and enjoyed nap time with her just as much as play time. Rumer immediately fell asleep, so exhausted from all she tried to do. I hope I've told Lee enough what a wonderful job she did.

CHAPTER 17

One of the most fun and useful things Lee taught Rumer was how to pose for pictures. Lee adorned Rumer in a variety of apparel when she babysat and had Rumer pose, capturing so many wonderful shots that we have of her. For any new bush planted or pretty flowers that bloomed, Lee plopped Rumer in front and had her pose as part of it. Lee asked her, "Rumer, is it okay if I take your picture?" It obviously was, for she wore sunglasses in one picture, a baseball cap in another, a sweatshirt specially cut out for her in another, and so on. You never knew what Lee would put on Rumer next.

Rumer was so shy at first, seeming to know that she was being captured in time, but later came to enjoy and even expect to be a part of any and all pictures. If she saw the camera and suspected pictures were in order, in she went, amongst a bunch of aunts, or with my grandmother in front of the flowers, or next to our cats, or in front of the birthday cake with the birthday person. She couldn't resist. Her whole life, every part, every aspect, was one that was a part of all of us, a part of our whole.

Lee can also take most of the credit for the vocabulary Rumer learned. One of Rumer's favorite words was "uppie," which meant anything from going upstairs to getting on the bed or couch to getting on the golf cart or in the car. "Find it" sent her searching intently for something we threw for her. She knew that when we said "hurry," she better high-tail it away from some bug or out of the way of some danger. "Run" was a step up from "hurry" as far as danger and she raced us to the house. She knew to stop and be still when we said, "Listen!" Or to proceed carefully when we told her, "Careful, Rumer."

And, she understood what strings of words meant, too, like: "Can I take your picture," "Tell your Mommies you're home," "Do you want to go downstairs," "All gone," "Wait a minute," and "I have something for you."

If we said, "Go around," she turned to go around the house to the other door rather than the one in which she asked to come. She knew that "I'll save you some" meant she got the last bite of what we were eating or the last drops of our coffee, so she was patient. She knew that "bed and snacks" meant to race upstairs to bed where a placemat full of snacks were waiting for her, mostly her vitamins, supplements, and eventually pain meds as she got older. She knew an uncountable number of words and phrases. She even knew some sign language, especially the sign for "more" and "I love you."

Lee taught and treated Rumer as a human child and told me that it got to the point where she didn't even have to say anything to Rumer. She just thought it and Rumer *knew*.

I believe this and believed their connection to be a special one (as Rumer had a special connection with each of us). It was especially apparent when Rumer was older and lived at my parents' during the daytime. She always knew when Lee was about 5 minutes from home, no matter what time it was, and suddenly got up from the couch to start looking out all the windows restlessly. Sure enough, about 5 minutes later, Lee pulled in the driveway and beeped a few times to announce herself. This sent Rumer into a frenzy of happy barking since Lee always had something for her. Hearing Lee's beeping, my family opened the front door, Rumer bursting out to greet Lee's car, barking with joy the whole way.

The two of them came into the house exuberantly together, Lee chattering to Rumer and Rumer panting and laughing. Rumer's head immediately dove into Lee's workbag, searching for her gifts. Sometimes it was a few French fries or a coveted piece of pizza crust. Lee gently handed the treat to Rumer, who took it oh-so-carefully in her front teeth. Lee told her, "These are for you Po-Po. Go to your spot." Rumer, looking at everyone she passed, laughing and wagging, proudly showing everyone what her Auntie Lee had given her, made her way to the living room rug so that she could lie down and enjoy her goodie. Her Auntie Lee never forgot her. Sometimes her gift was a new ball, or a new toy to tear apart—she never knew for sure—but she always counted on something. Showing her complete appreciation, she never failed to thank her Auntie Lee and always remembered to go back and kiss her after each and every gift.

Rumer was not only very intelligent, but she was also just so in-tune to all of us, and all of us in-tune to her. She was so "knowing" that it was hard *not* treating her like a person.

CHAPTER 18

After Rumer came into our lives, Cheryl and I were very interested in reading even more about pit bulls and learning as much as we could about them. We purchased numerous books, paid for a subscription to "*The Pit Bull Gazette*," and looked up as much information on the Colby line, the line from which Rumer came, as we could. Everything we read just reinforced all the information we had researched previously: pit bulls, maybe admired for their gameness (which only means tenacity for sticking with something) have been traditionally bred to be the most human-friendly breed of dog. We found this out first-hand with Rumer, who only wanted to be with people, with us, who only wanted to be the center of our world.

Lee's early bonds with Rumer enhanced this connectedness between her and the rest of us. Rumer was part of the family, treated as a child, and even dressed accordingly for get-togethers. Cheryl and I had great fun dressing Rumer for all of these occasions. The fact that she loved and expected to be a part of the family made this even more special. She undoubtedly knew that she was an integral and most important piece in our puzzle and loved nothing more than when Cheryl and I prepared her in her costumes.

On Thanksgiving, we put a feather band around her head, bracelets of beads around her legs, and makeup on her face, dressed as a Native American. On Christmas, she wore beautiful velvet collars and bells; on birthdays, she wore a birthday hat. Even on football playoff days, she wore the jersey of the team for which Paul rooted. She *loved* showing off these outfits, laughing her pit bull laugh the whole time in good humor.

One get-together, Cheryl and I painted Rumer's toenails with red nail polish, thinking that it would make her look pretty. However, after watching her prance around with gory red nails, even Cheryl and I had to admit that it didn't look quite right. Although she let us do this, we never did it again. In all honesty, it looked a little freakish.

Halloween was always the most fun. We went through many years of dressing Rumer differently, my family always eagerly waiting to see her. It was so much fun for Cheryl and me to plan everything, to sit Rumer in front of us and dress her in her costume. Stuffing her legs in shirt arms, head into shirt openings, Rumer never minded how Cheryl and I contorted her body in order to get her into her outfit.

Her first year, she was a pirate complete with a plastic sword in her belt. Cheryl and I rented a child's pirate outfit and cut a place out for her tail. After the party, my mother had to sew the slit together again before we returned it. The next year, she was a bumblebee. For some reason, this outfit really embarrassed her. We had a big party that year which included my aunts and uncles and many of my parents' friends. Rumer did not want to come out of the bedroom where we dressed her and, when forced, hung her head in shame. This was the one and only outfit she refused to keep on, forcing us to remove it.

Another year, Cheryl designed a graveyard between our barn and front brook. It was complete with a decapitated corpse rearing out of the ground, blood spraying from its severed artery, tombstones, and other scary items. There was Rumer, posing in the middle, fake blood and mud smeared all over her.

Cheryl actually made the best Halloween outfit for Rumer herself one year, spending countless hours one night fitting, cutting, and painting it. Rumer watched Cheryl curiously as she measured and cut, tongue bitten in concentration, her face transforming from a frown into a widening smile as it all came together. As she worked, she asked Rumer quite often to stand up so that she could measure and fit it to her some more.

Rumer was so patient, standing up over and over again for hours in order for Cheryl to perfect her creation. The outfit in making was a replica of a racecar that Paul used to drive. Paul had raced a modified stock car at Riverside Park Raceway in Agawam. A Six Flags Park has since taken over what was once a small, family-owned amusement park, and they did away with the racetrack, to everyone's dismay. Cheryl was particularly proud of this outfit since it turned out to be an unbelievably true miniature replica of what Paul's car really looked like. Rumer wore the "car" over her back and even had a bandana tied around her head to make it look as though she was wearing a helmet.

It was a smash! She was so much fun!

CHAPTER 19

As part of our preparation in getting a dog, Cheryl and I had done a lot of research on different kinds of dog training. We had such dreams and ideals as to what we wanted to do with Rumer, dreaming of training her to be the best "dog," a perfect pit bull ambassador. One type of training that kept popping up as very interesting was called Schuntzhund.

Schuntzhund is a highly disciplined form of training which contains three parts: tracking, obedience, and protection. The word Schuntzhund itself is a German word meaning "protection dog." It was developed in Germany specifically for the German Shepherd dog in order to test whether the German Shepherd acted and performed in a manner for which the breed was intended, testing the dog specifically for police work. We decided to contact a trainer in the area who used the Schuntzhund method in order to find out more about it.

When we called the trainer, we informed him that we had a pit bull. He told us that he would be starting his classes on Saturdays that first fall we had Rumer, the fall of 1992, and that we could bring Rumer to the first class to see what it was like.

The first Saturday of the training finally arrived and the three of us excitedly began our journey to the UMASS Amherst football field where the Schuntzhund class was taking place. Rumer knew something was up and happily watched out the front window from the passenger seat the whole 45 minutes, anxiously awaiting what was to come.

As we pulled into the parking area and clipped Rumer's leash on to walk toward the training area, the trainer came over to greet us. Very young and handsome with a well-built body showing through his Schuntzhund windbreaker, he introduced himself and knelt down to pet Rumer's head. He talked to us a little about his training method and was nice enough to give us some excellent pointers on training Rumer ourselves.

Fondling the choke collar we had on her, he said, "This is way too thick for her. It's just slamming her every time you pull it. You don't want to do that. The chain should be finer for a neck her size."

He then walked us over to the group and had us begin by just watching a few people work their dogs, all of which were German Shepherds. The sound of whistles greeted us as we approached the training area, then silence as everyone watched one shepherd go through his obstacles, the only sound a slight whooshing as owner and shepherd raced through the dew-covered grass. We continued, watching the obedience maneuvers, the dogs listening intently to the cues of their owners. The agility maneuvers came next, the dogs agilely clawing their way up and over the various obstacles.

The beauty of the dogs and their accomplishments was undeniable and Cheryl and I murmured to each other in appreciation of the difficulty of their actions and the show of such discipline. As we stood there, I realized how proud I was of Rumer, how proud I was with her at my side. She was my compact, muscular little girl and oh-so-perfectly beautiful. She was so good that day taking in all the action, activity, and excitement with the patience of one much more mature. She seemed a little intimidated by so many large dogs, as she was still a youngster and looked so small next to the shepherds, but certainly watched with bold curiosity and interest.

After everything we learned that day, and after doing more research in the following weeks, we came to realize what we hadn't before. Schuntzhund is not only obedience, but also a practice for training attack dogs or police dogs. Pit bulls, being an exceptionally human-friendly breed, do not generally do well at this training. It is very difficult training them to attack a person. Shepherds, on the other hand, are bred for this type of protective work. For these reasons, Cheryl and I decided against Schuntzhund for our training.

Regardless of how it all turned out and the decision we ultimately made, that morning was beautiful. It was bright and sunny, so we took full advantage of being out with Rumer. Cheryl and I posed with Rumer for pictures on the pristine, green football field, something we had not yet done. We took our time and walked the property, all of us enjoying the sights, sounds, and smells of college in the fall: young, healthy adults in full physical bloom, whistles, yells, the activities of various sports. After enjoying the morning together, we went home.

The experience was very interesting to me and I was glad that we had pursued learning more about Schuntzhund. It has always been my lifelong desire to learn anything and everything there is to know about animals.

CHAPTER 20

As that first fall turned colder bringing sleet and bitter weather, skies gray and pregnant with snow, Cheryl and I decided to make our family a little larger. This first winter with Rumer, we decided to get a horse.

I have always loved horses and had hoped beyond hope that I could have them in my life again some day. Cheryl knew this and always supported my desire. However, I know how much time it takes to keep horses so I planned on waiting until I finished my master's degree before I seriously thought about getting one. The planning was fun, though. Cheryl and I visited a variety of horse farms that summer, my interests ranging from Arabians to Morgans to Andalusians, a beautiful Spanish breed.

One day at work I was reading an advertisement in *Horse Illustrated* magazine for a farm that bred Hispano-Arabes. These horses are a combination of the Arabian and the Andalusian. I couldn't imagine the beauty of such a creature. Curiosity and love of all that is *horse* prompted me to call the farm and get more information. The woman who ran the farm answered my call and was extremely friendly. After chatting with her and asking all my questions, she invited Cheryl and me to visit her place. She informed me that she had four horses for sale, ranging in ages from two years to four months. Since the farm was located only 2 ½ hours away in Sharon, Cheryl and I decided to make an appointment on one of our vacation days that summer.

When we drove to the farm that day, I couldn't wait to arrive. I was so excited as we pulled down the driveway and my jaw dropped open as I caught my first glimpse of the astoundingly elegant horses. Frisky at our arrival, they pranced and ran around the paddock, their full, black manes and tails lifted by the wind. I was particularly drawn to one, an Arabian/Andalusian filly who was 4 ½ months old, her name EEA Princesa. Cheryl and I both fell in love with her that day. She took to following Cheryl around the paddock with her head hanging over Cheryl's shoulder, curiosity and intelligence reflected in her gorgeous brown eyes. She would suddenly sprint off in excitement, tiny round hooves barely touching the ground before they were back in the air, prancing and dancing her way around the paddock with her little tail straight up in the air as if waving to these interesting new humans. The sassiness and freedom of her spirit captured my heart. We left the farm that day and continued to look at other horses and visit other farms throughout the next few months, but I couldn't stop thinking about this little dark bay filly that had the refined beauty of a carousel horse. I planned on saving as diligently as I could in order to afford her.

As winter quickly approached, Cheryl said to me one day, "Why wait to get your horse, Honey? I know it's always on your mind. Just get one now. You love them; just get one."

Does anyone wonder why I love her so much? Enter our little Hispano-Arabe, EEA Princesa, or "Cesa," into our lives.

As soon as we made the decision to buy Cesa, we began the arduous task of going through all the variables involved in purchasing her. In the middle of all of our planning, tragedy struck Cesa's present owner at the farm. That year, she had bred her first purebred Andalusian colt and had great plans for him. He was to be her foundation sire for the rest of her breedings. He was only a few months old when he was attacked and killed one night by neighborhood dogs, the attack and horrible death witnessed by the other horses on the farm, including Cesa. The woman was understandably distraught over this colt's death and couldn't decide on which direction to go as a breeder, or if she even wanted to sell Cesa. Cheryl and I waited patiently. After a few weeks, Cesa's breeder finally called. She decided to sell her.

Cheryl and I spent the next few busy weeks refinancing our home for the money to build our barn, put up our fence, and purchase this expensive little baby. Paul's girlfriend Katie grew up with and currently had horses. Her brother-in-law Gerry was a carpenter and knew the importance of having a safe and well-built barn. That November, we discussed plans with him and he agreed to build the beautiful barn we have today.

As Gerry and his helper built through Thanksgiving that year and into the first week of December, Rumer loved going out every morning to help them. The two men arrived very early and bundled warmly, only their faces visible peeking out from their hoods, nature already portending a very cold winter. Rumer just couldn't wait to get out to them, skipping her breakfast to hurry outside. This was probably when her love for coffee began. Before the men started working and again during their morning break, Rumer sat between them as if a part of their group to share their morning coffee and some scraps of doughnuts. After their breakfast break, I heard Rumer begin her barking for the men's attention. Looking out the window occasionally to monitor the goings on, I saw her skinny vanilla body wearing my pink sweatshirt specially cut out to fit her, jumping and diving around the men, barking and pointing out her stick in order to entice them to play.

Gerry asked me one cold day, the skeleton of a new barn barely revealing the masterpiece it would be, if we were sure that Rumer was a pure pit bull. He said, "I don't think she is full pit. I think that's wrong. Do you have papers for her?"

I said to Gerry, "Really, I know she's skinny and doesn't look it, but, yes, we do have the registration papers for Rumer as an American Pit Bull Terrier."

He shook his head and muttered about the truth of this.

I understood his skepticism. Many people had already mistaken her for a yellow lab or a boxer. I suppose that keeping her ears natural and not docking them as most people do with pit bulls did make her look less traditional. But, we were adamant about keeping her ears in their natural condition and would never dock any of our dogs' ears. We have learned how to tell so much about what they're feeling, what they need, or what they're trying to say with their ears, if they're sick or sad or frisky or just shy. Rumer's ears were perfect, folding back to her head just right, folds of creamy velvet with a hint of black just framing the edges.

Our barn was finished in early December. We hired Blue Chip Horse Transportation to pick up our new baby and bring her to us the weekend of December 12, 1992. My family and some friends came for the occasion. Even our old neighbor Toby, wondering at the buzz of activity, walked over to be a part of the greeting committee.

Cesa arrived without incident, a fat, little, dark 6-month-old filly that looked like a donkey, mane and tail shaved completely off in the Andalusian tradition, as they are typically kept for their first year of life. I watched nervously as she was calmly led down the ramp of the trailer. Cesa was so good and so smart even as a baby, careful of her footing going down the ramp and into the icy snow, walking so confidently into her new paddock and barn as if she had finally come home.

With Cesa tucked safely into her fresh stall, family and friends joined Cheryl and me while we surrounded our new baby. We popped open a bottle of champagne and toasted future happiness with Cesa, forming a circle of love around which Cesa was the sole object of wondrous, complete affection. Arabians are known not only for their intelligence, but also for their affinity to people, often sharing the tents of their owners in their desert homeland. Cesa revealed, from the very beginning, this wonderful Arabian trait.

After Cesa came to live with us, our elderly neighbor Toby was a new person. She loved horses and came to visit Cesa often. Her very old Morgan horse Corky grazed in the field bordering our properties, a mere 20 feet and some thin electric wiring separating him from Cesa. He and Cesa were in love. I sat in the thick grass chewing on a sweet green sprig as when I was a child, brilliant yellow buttercups surrounding us, and watched Cesa, appreciating that I had a horse in my life once again. Most of the time, Cesa made sure she had Corky in her sights, whether following him along the fence line or just standing for hours, staring at him. This old fellow who couldn't see, hear, or walk well, back swayed and hooves cracked with age, was the object of such intense adoration. If he had only known!

CHAPTER 21

The Christmas of 1992, Rumer's first with us, my family, Cheryl, and I made plans to go to Bright Nights in Springfield. Bright Nights is a special event occurring only around Christmastime. A winding road takes one slowly through a brilliant display of different Christmas-themed statues spaced out along the route, constructed of multi- colored Christmas lights. When we all planned to go, there was no question that Rumer was coming with us.

On a blustery, wintry night before Christmas, seven of us along with Cheryl, Katie, and Rumer piled into my mother's Mazda van. We barely fit and most of us were seated unsafely and uncomfortably. I think Rumer was the only one who was comfortable, sitting in her prime spot in the passenger seat with Grammie who was holding her protectively and lovingly on her lap.

I, stuck in the way back of the van and trying to keep my claustrophobia at bay, watched expectantly as my father drove up to the entrance. There, he was approached by the welcoming elf, paid our fee to enter, and began to drive along the meandering road toward the beautiful displays of lights. Even Rumer, quiet and curious, sat still the whole time, watching in wonder with the rest of us. She seemed to understand what we were observing, happy to be a part of our family outing, and then slept soundly all the way home, knowing the event was through. It was just never an option to not include her in whatever we did.

Christmas Day came with its frenzy of gift giving. I think Rumer received more gifts than all the rest of my family combined. Foregoing opening my own presents, I watched her excitement like a proud mother, it being Rumer's very first Christmas. She didn't seem to know which

59

toy or chewie to work on first, and stopped to bark in excitement every once in a while or shred some abandoned wrapping paper. I felt more joy in seeing her happiness than any present could give me.

After Christmas, winter began to pass quickly and February 7th arrived, bringing Rumer's first birthday. Cheryl, my family, and I threw a big party for her that Sunday. Rumer posed for pictures in her birthday hat—how patient she was as my mother tried to get the perfect shots—and was showered with…more presents!

As spring approached, she and I looked even more forward to our walks around the property every day. Only now, she wasn't that little baby any more that tired so easily. Now she was bigger and stronger and had an endless amount of energy. We had to make a few circuits of the property to appease her, but I never tired of watching her bound about, smelling, digging, chasing. She was like a sawhorse, so energy-bound that she ran in an up and down manner, her skinny shape bursting to let loose in mischief and fun. Her eyes aglitter, she looked back at me occasionally, still always checking.

I threw sticks for her to chase at various intervals and she always found a huge limb to drag back to me, so big that she ran sideways in order to pull it. Rumer growled and struggled to get it back to me, her lanky young body in a "U" from the effort. Ever hopeful, she dropped this much-too-heavy limb at my feet, looked up at me to throw it, and danced around the limb expectantly. She loved her body at this time and loved what this new, strong body could do. She was so agile and tireless, so confident in her ability to do anything.

We had such a different kind of fun from the fun we had when she was a small baby, that small baby at whom I would just stare in wonder, in appreciation, that bundle of joy and happiness of which I was so protective. Now, Rumer's joy was tangible, an aura you could almost wonderingly catch and savor, her energy and love of life so bursting forth and overflowing that one couldn't help but be affected by it.

How couldn't I laugh at this clown, her head buried in the sand, sneezing as she surfaced from the grains she inhaled up her nose in her exuberance? How couldn't I laugh at her frenzied digging, stopping to sniff and snort, then digging even deeper, sand flying up and out between her skinny back legs, her tail curled up like a monkey? How couldn't I feel joy in seeing her laughing face as she ran and dodged through the grass, so proud of her power; or to see her diving in the pond for a stick, ducking her head all the way under the water only to come up sputtering and sneezing with her treasured limb; or the way she manipulated from me one more lap of walking the property; or of the way she had to occasionally come back to me, even amidst all of this fun, just to kiss me and show me how much she loved me? How couldn't I have such joy in the presence of this ray of pure light? How couldn't I love life with just as much enthusiasm and passion as that which this little soul showed me?

Even at this young age, Rumer taught me so much about life and how to live, how precious such moments are, and how happy we should be for them. My heart couldn't have been more full of love for her, more full for all the gifts she constantly gave to me, more full for all of which she constantly reminded me.

At some point on our walks, we invariably stopped at a pond that Rumer grew to love. This pond seemed to have been placed by divine guidance, perfectly dropped in the middle of the field that would eventually separate my parents' house from mine. It boasted cool, clear water surrounded by boulders larger than we were and cozily nestled in by a few pines. The red-winged blackbirds that lived here greeted us with their peculiar, lovely sound, like that of trickling water, as we approached.

Rumer ran to the pond and jumped on the biggest, highest boulder, head flicking back and forth immediately, a perfect lookout point from which to glimpse any floating stick or wayward ball. She made such a beautiful picture, with the clear pond reflecting both her image and the boulders on which she crouched. She was in the middle of her skinny teenage "awkward" stage, but still so beautiful. Her black facial features stood out so darkly and deeply and her brown eyes were intense, outlined in the black mascara that surrounded them. Cheryl captured a fantastic picture of her that summer as she stood on one of those boulders. We took this picture to the local mall soon after in order to have it put on a mug as a gift for Lee. The man who was working that particular booth in the mall offered us $500 on the spot for Rumer. She was that stunning, but of course we said no.

That summer, Lee asked Rumer if she could use her paw to make a paw print in a cement mixture. Rumer happily agreed. Once the print hardened, Lee posted it by the edge of this pond where it still stands, along with Lee's hand-made sign that proclaims the area "Rumer's Pond".

CHAPTER 22

Spring approached, along with the excitement of birds, the chickadees with their spring song that epitomized the beginning of such a glorious season, the finches turning a brilliant yellow, the swallow couple that inhabited our barn every year swooping in with their typical exuberance. In came the bursting of tree buds, flowers and greenery that just can't help but brighten one's mood. In came "Rumer Rebellious."

In striking contrast to that cute, obedient little puppy, Rumer underwent an incredibly rebellious stage. That puppy that loved to please us, to be near us, to obey our every command, suddenly grew into a lanky, defiant teenager. Rumer now ignored every word Cheryl and I said, every command we tried to wield. She knew what we were asking of her, but pretended not to. Cheryl and I tried calling her to come in, she looked in the opposite direction in utter disregard. We went after her, she ran the other way. We tried to surround her and she hid behind a tree, her butt and tail sticking out, thinking she couldn't be seen because she couldn't see us. And, when we got close enough to grab her, off she ran in one of her favorite areas, through the fields surrounding our property where the grass and clover grew taller than she, a grounded dolphin, diving and jumping, running and ducking.

We watched her in complete frustration, but in reality, it was a beautiful sight. Laughing in fun and mischief, ears back and flat to her head with mouth wide open, grabbing at anything in her path, she leaped and ran, joyous with her life and newfound freedom in outrunning us. All we saw was her head as she made her leaps. The rest of the time, the tall grasses hid her, her place revealed only by the frantic waving of grass and clover stalks in her wake. But, she was maddening in her rebellion. She could certainly outrun us now and we could never catch her.

It was awful. We thought, "Where is that mall guy now?" We joked that we would take a nickel for her, even entertaining the idea of giving her away. Her Auntie Lee always jumped on this joke, often asking Cheryl or me with the deepest of sincerity, "Can I have her? I'll give you a million dollars for her." Lee was forever in love with this little soul.

Cheryl and I plugged on through that spring and into summer, wondering what we had gotten into, wondering if this was how it was going to be our whole life with Rumer. If so, she was going to drive us mad.

Then, suddenly, we all went to bed one night toward the end of that summer, woke up the next morning, and... she listened. The transformation was so obvious and clear-cut, it's memorable to this day. One day we had a rebellious, disobedient teenager, the next, we called her and... she actually came, trotting up to us, black eyebrows raised with an inquiring expression that reminded me of that good puppy of a year ago.

Cheryl and I looked at each other in wonder. We shook our heads and mumbled that this must be a passing thing, a mistake, this new-found obedience, so we tested her a little and took her for a walk. She stayed with us. We came back from our walk and went into the house. She came in when we asked, walking in through the screen door that I held open for her as if saying, "What are you looking at? This is how I always listen!"

Hmmm. We couldn't believe it. Cheryl and I just started getting used to the fact that we were stuck with an obstinate, stubborn pit bull. But suddenly, she was just... good. And, good she stayed from that moment on. It was as if a switch had been turned on (or off). She was thereafter the angel we came to know, her teenage stage becoming a distant, even funny memory. Thank goodness!

CHAPTER 23

Since purchasing the property in Southampton in 1977, my parents often discussed selling our house in Feeding Hills in order to move. As kids, we dreaded "the talk." Our goal was to finish school in Feeding Hills where we had always lived and had our friends. But, as we grew older, we realized how golden the property in Southampton was and how lucky we really were. After Cheryl and I built our house, my parents began to talk more seriously about moving to join us.

To Cheryl's and my delight, it was the next summer that my parents finally decided to partake in the "big move." I believe Rumer was really the deciding factor. They loved her so very much and wanted to be near her.

As part of the planning, my family came to Southampton every weekend. When they arrived, we all walked to the area where their house would be built. At that time, the property looked nothing like the beautiful place it is now. We found ourselves climbing over or carefully avoiding many obstacles including deep ravines, downed trees, and junk, even old rusted cars that others had dumped on the land long ago. It has only been due to my father's hard work with his bulldozer and creative imagination that we have what it is today.

When we finally made it to the back corner of the property, my father found a stick to draw out in the sand where the house would sit. Rumer always accompanied us, so happy to have everyone together. She showed off, like a child, demonstrating to everyone how well she knew the property and how she could lead them anywhere they would like to go. She was a complete clown whose goal was to make everyone laugh. She thought she was especially funny when she snuck up on my father, leapt straight up in the air, and stole the stick out of his hand. She ran with it, where, once a safe distance away, she proceeded to shred it. Or, to be even funnier, she dug wherever my father tried to draw in the sand, completely ruining his designs. To Rumer's delight, we laughed as my father exclaimed his familiar, "That dog!"

It was one of Rumer's favorite things, to dig in the nice soft sand on this hill, overjoyed to be able to dig so deep. The front portion of her was completely out of our sight, just her back end and curled monkey tail visible. She dug and dug, ears full of dirt, nose completely covered, eyebrows peppered with sand whenever she breached to show herself again, making us all laugh at her clown-like look. She was so happy.

Funny dog, making us laugh all the time, so happy and content when dirty. Sandy sheets, sleeping between Cheryl and me—always. Every time you put your head on one of our pillows, it is invariably with your ear flap up, as we always joked dirty ears-that-were-never-cleaned juice smearing our clean pillow cases. How I didn't care, spooning you from behind, once in a while throughout the night kissing the back of your sandy head that smelled like earth, sun, and fresh air. I breathe you in with the deepest breaths, making everything you are a part of me...how I love that. There is nothing I could possibly love more.

CHAPTER 24

Monnie, our youngest cat, was very fond of the back corner of the property on which my family built their house. When Rumer and I took our morning walks and approached this area, Monnie heard us and crawled out from under some old boards that my father had stacked up, yawning and stretching, blinking cutely at us in the slanted rays of the morning sun while acting as if she just left the most comfortable bed in the world. She came trotting up to us, tail straight in the air, the slight kink in its carmel-colored tip the only bend, sniffed noses with Rumer in greeting, and turned to come along with us for the rest of our walk.

Every once in a while, Monnie got frisky and ran ahead to jump on a big boulder. There, she sat to wait for us to catch up, tail swishing with impatience. Rumer still loved to tease Monnie so chased her to the boulder, got down in her play pose, and barked at Monnie with her bratty, teasing bark. It never took much to infuriate Monnie, and this certainly proved a most effective way. Monnie threatened Rumer by raising one front paw in warning but Rumer never did take the hint. She loved this game, ducking and jumping about, circling the rock, every once in a while grabbing Monnie's bushy tail on her way around. This circling put Monnie at a constant disadvantage, ears flat to her head in anger, growling in fury, she tried to swat Rumer. When Monnie finally tired of the game, she jumped off the rock and continued on our walk. Rumer always accepted Monnie's choice of when to end the game, happy to just go back to sniffing and poking around on her own, finding just as much fun herself.

This "game" continued well into their old age. Diane and Lee, when seeing it in action, often asked Rumer, " Ru, why don't you leave Monnie alone today?" But, we really think that Monnie liked this game, too, even though she pretended not to.

Monnie continued home with us to eat before heading off on her own again. She sometimes stopped just long enough to pick a fight with Taja or Lily, aggressively reinforcing her status as "boss." Cheryl and I always counted it as a blessing that she chose the back area of the property as her own. This, for the most part, kept her away from Taja, who preferred our barn and hayloft, and Lily, who preferred the house. Cheryl and I always suspected that Toby fed Taja once in a while, since she occasionally came home smelling like tuna or bacon. When she did decide to sleep in the house, she left a mess of dirt, leaf remnants, and other outdoor debris wherever she curled up. She had the cutest, smartest personality.

It was actually due to Taja that our barn was saved from burning down one winter evening. That particular night, it was extremely cold, the kind of below zero night that made your bones ache seconds after you step out the door. Due to this cold, Taja decided to sleep inside. Suddenly, in the middle of the night, she woke Cheryl by pawing the side door in the kitchen instead of the front door, frantic to go out. Cheryl, by going to the kitchen area to let her out, was able to see the fire outside the kitchen window that faced the barn.

We later found out that the fire was caused when the heating element, used to keep the horses' water from freezing, touched the plastic trough in which it sat. The trough then started to melt, eventually catching on fire. Once Cheryl spotted the fire, she called anxiously for me to help while she ran out in her pajamas, grabbing the fire extinguisher as she went. As I ran outside, the cold licking at my exposed ankles, I saw Cheryl's silhouette haloed by the bright orange flames reaching toward our barn, the horses nervously nickering. Thank goodness for Cheryl's quick thinking. She put the fire out by herself within a few seconds and saved our horses. And, thank goodness for Taja, waking her in the first place.

Our sweet, gentle soul Lily was mostly our indoor cat. I'm sure this fact helped prevent many a fight with Monnie. She was uninterested in going out unless the family and Rumer were outside to protect her. Otherwise, she stayed inside, the pristine white of her paws hardly ever dirtied by the outdoors. I think she only ventured to my parents' area once or twice. In all honesty, she was afraid of Monnie too, though she was twice Monnie's size.

Though Cheryl and I loved Monnie as much as all our other babies, she was a miniature gray terror, best on her own and away from the other cats. She, the smallest, invariably started all the fights, tormenting Taja and Lily horrendously in her frustration at having to share her home with other animals. She tolerated Rumer, but still established herself as boss. We often caught them cuddled so sweetly, Monnie lying against Rumer's soft, warm belly, both settling in for a nap. Sometimes, Monnie kindly tended to Rumer and held Rumer still while she cleaned Rumer's face and neck with great determination. But, without warning she might suddenly turn this sweet moment into an attack, digging her claws into Rumer's chest while sinking her teeth into Rumer's throat. Rumer always calmly waited until Monnie released her after which, Monnie jumped away and trotted off, tail flicking back and forth, ears flat with rage. Rumer never took offense, but accepted this little cat's schizophrenia with the patience of a saint.

So, it was with great relief to Cheryl and me that Monnie claimed the back corner of the property as hers. When my father began building their house during the fall of 1994, Monnie was always there, watching and monitoring each stage. My father loved having her around, since she acted more like a dog than a cat. She kept him company all day, walking amidst the chaos of construction, making sure the house was on schedule, waiting patiently for my family to move in and "release" her from the "awful" living conditions that Cheryl and I offered. She seemed to know that my family was coming and, as if it were the most natural thing in the world, just moved in along with them when everything was finished. Of course, they fulfilled her most important requirement: *No Other Animals*. She became attached to and enamored with Lee most of all who administered to her solely and completely. Lee brushed her, held and cooed to her like a baby, and shared her bed with this little sergeant, often kissing her cute, gray cheeks and hugging her tightly to her chest with love.

She visited us once in a while, sauntering down the gravel road to our house in a swirl of determination, ready to torment Taja and Lily, responsible for giving Lily numerous abscesses from her scratches or bites. But, for the most part, she packed her bags and never came back. We all watched her little gray butt, kinked tail switching in a last show of irritation, disappear down the drive, little puffs of dust thrown behind each determined step, and breathed a sigh of relief. Her relationship with Rumer became much deeper and more loving when Rumer began to spend her days at my parents' house. They became very good company for each other, Monnie not threatened since Rumer was "just a dog," and Rumer loved her sisters, no matter their temperaments.

CHAPTER 25

My family moved in and thus began our most beautiful life. Rumer now had everything she wanted. She loved my family so much that there was nothing else in the world she had to experience or see outside of our boundaries. In came my family and out came "Rumer, Master Manipulator."

We should have seen it coming, the budding commander-in-general she became, when, in 1994, my family decided to vacation in Florida for 10 days at Christmas. While the rest of us were gone, Paul and Katie were to stay at my house to take care of Rumer, Cesa, and the cats while Rob stayed at my parents' house. With everything settled, we excitedly set off with high hopes for fun and sun!

If anyone's ever driven from Massachusetts to Florida, one knows how grueling this drive can be. We drove in two cars, my parents and Diane in one with Lee, Cheryl and I in the other. When we made the decision to drive, we all made a safety pact that there would always be two people per car awake at one time: the driver, of course, and the occupier of the passenger seat, whose job it was to help the driver. Also, Cheryl had major narcoleptic problems at that time, often having to stop on her way home from work (a ½ hour drive) in order to take a 15-minute nap. She made it a condition of the trip that she not be a driver, obviously! Unfortunately, the drive was so grueling that everyone in our car was wiped out by the time we reached Georgia. Even by New Jersey, I was hallucinating, thinking that I had gone through a tollbooth at 70 miles per hour without noticing!

At 3:30 am, we pulled into a gas station in Georgia. Lee and I, both beyond exhaustion, woke Cheryl and told her she had to drive.

So good-natured, Cheryl popped up and said, "Okay." We propped her up in the driver's seat, I was the passenger, and Lee, who said, "Oh, I'll never be able to sleep," began snoring before we even pulled out of the station. We continued south, Diane driving my parents' car behind us with my father as her passenger.

After a few minutes on the highway, Diane noticed our car start to weave. She said, "Dad, do you see that?" He answered, "Yeah, try to get their attention!"

They didn't have any luck getting our attention, for good reason. Lee was asleep in the back, I was asleep in the passenger seat, and Cheryl was sound asleep in the driver's seat! There just comes a time when you become so tired that you don't care what happens to you, you just want to sleep. Even at the risk of my life, I couldn't stay awake!

The ridges on the sides of the highway saved our lives. After Cheryl fell asleep, she weaved over to the left, woke up and straightened the car, then, fell asleep again and weaved over to the right, crossing the ridges. The sound of these bumps woke her and she hastily pulled into the next rest stop.

Poor Cheryl. Of course, it was our fault for putting her in such a position. But, everyone jumped on her at once anyway: "How could you fall asleep?!"…"What were you thinking?!"… our yelling intermingled, magnified in the predawn stillness. Once we all stopped talking, exhausted, Cheryl admitted to having a full-fledged dream! That confession brought another round of yelling and arguing. After we all settled down, we continued on our way to the elusive Florida with Cheryl now safely tucked in the back to sleep.

We reached Florida to find that the state was in the middle of one of the coldest snaps that could be remembered. We spent a few cold (in the 30's) and rainy days in Orlando. Instead of fun and sun, we spent most of our money purchasing heavy coats (which we didn't pack, thinking it wouldn't be necessary) and winter hats. My father bought his hat in one of Disney's country villages; a green, woolen thing that looked like Peter Pan's hat, but which we all envied for its apparent warmth.

After a few days spent at rainy Epcot and Universal Studios, we headed south to Sarasota where my parents owned a beautiful little condominium. We *were* able to go to the beach, although fully clothed for the cold, and the sun *did* shine. The only problem was that we all started to get ill from our marathon drive and our days in Orlando.

Sick and defeated, we decided to travel back home early, even after hearing the weather reports of a major winter storm heading toward the east. This storm coincided perfectly with the day of our departure but we just wanted to get home so desperately that we were willing to risk life and limb. We missed the rest of the family and we missed Rumer terribly. We learned a very important lesson on this trip: holidays and special occasions just weren't the same without Rumer. Life wasn't life without Rumer.

So we made the emotional decision to head back home and, unfortunately, hit every storm as we traveled north. Icy roads in Georgia and the Carolinas caused traffic accidents, sliding of cars, jackknifing of trucks, and more vehicles in ditches than on the roads. The more north we slowly went, the more we hit major snowfall. As we approached New Jersey, the heavy snow caused traffic to travel bumper-to-bumper at under 5 miles per hour on the highway. Thick, wet, heavy flakes were coming down so quickly that it was too difficult to see. At this point, we realized that we needed to stop for the night or risk our lives unnecessarily. Although sorely disappointed, we stopped at the next hotel.

We awoke the next morning to an overcrowded, chaotic hotel, but all was brighter and better and we continued home without incident. When we finally reached our street, Cheryl and I almost wept with gratitude. We got our second wind after pulling in the driveway, excited to see Rumer. I just couldn't wait to hug and kiss her. We both yearned for the comfort and love and joy that she would certainly bestow upon us, having missed us for so long.

Oh, how wrong we were! I opened the front door as Cheryl and I exclaimed with joy, "Rumer, we're home!" I knelt down, arms wide open, expectantly awaiting her running body to knock me over with exuberant dog glee. But, she jumped off the couch, looked at us in surprise, then meandered by and out the front door, glaring in total disdain as she went. She looked so disgusted with the both of us, whether for being back or for having left in the first place, I still don't know.

Many miles, many sicknesses, many luckily-missed-accidents, and about 500 Advil amongst us later, Cheryl and I felt our joy at being back with Rumer dwindle to sadness. She wasn't even happy to see us! It actually took her three to four days to warm to us again. I was so devastated by this that I vowed to never leave her again. My heart couldn't bear it!

To this day, both Cheryl and I have never been away from home since—not even one night! How such little effort it took for Rumer to attain her role of Master Manipulator.

CHAPTER 26

In the spring of 1995, Cheryl and I decided to purchase a pool for our whole family's enjoyment. After reviewing the many options, we decided on an on-side pool, one which is placed into a slope. Since our back yard sloped down and away from our house, one side of the pool met the slope and was almost "underground" while the far side was 10 feet or so off the ground. My father generously offered to build a deck that surrounded the whole pool. It turned out to be a beautiful setup.

Rumer helped my father build this deck throughout that spring when she turned three. She sat or lay in the grass on the slope overlooking the pool, content to be outside in the shady back yard with him. She enjoyed my father's company and the spring sunshine, the different, bright lightness to the air, and the first warm breezes from the south. Performing her very important duty, she protected her land as my father measured and sawed, his hammering echoing peacefully from the woods. My father took breaks during the day to sit down next to her, side by side on the warming grass, both of them enjoying the beautiful spring weather and activity.

Cheryl and I came home after work, excited to see the progress, my father just as excited to show us. As we surveyed his work, my father exclaimed, "That dog! She's so funny. I'll sit there next to her (pointing to the spot they shared under a nice shady tree) and stare at her, just to see what she'll do. And, you know what? She's too busy to look at me. Even if I lean in close and kiss her, she just keeps watch! She'll even pretend to see something and do her fake 'wuff' at something made-up, just to make sure I get the hint to leave her alone to her duties." He shook his head and laughed, thinking Rumer was so funny.

They did this every day, buddies, until my father's beautiful deck was finished. We all enjoyed the pool and this deck so much that hot summer, not realizing the one big problem with decks…bees. Unbeknownst to us, a very large wasp nest began to thrive under the boards where we relaxed on our towels. Rumer, on her own towel, slept next to us in the hot sun, loving to bake.

One afternoon she got stung as she walked across the deck. She yelped a little and bit at the sting in her paw, but otherwise seemed okay when we meticulously checked her over, Lee anxiously attending to her and kissing her paw better. A few minutes later, as Paul pulled down the driveway to leave, Rumer ran to his car, barking for him to see her. Paul stopped, got out of the car, knelt down to say 'bye' to her and…suddenly, Rumer collapsed, right in his arms. She was in shock, allergic to the bee sting.

It was a Sunday afternoon, so Cheryl and I realized with dismay that we had to go to Springfield where the closest emergency vet was located. Paul picked up Rumer's limp body and placed her across the back seat of our car, my family watching in quiet distress. I jumped in the driver's seat as Cheryl got in the back, desperately holding on to Rumer. I clicked on the emergency flashers and began the 45-minute drive as fast as I safely could, Cheryl's urgent pleas encouraging me from the back seat.

During the entire drive, Rumer was completely limp and barely breathing. Cheryl and I were terribly frightened and in utter disbelief that Rumer was fading away due to such an insignificant thing. It really looked as though we were losing her. I was driving as fast as I could, but the drive seemed to take forever and I had the sinking feeling that we were never going to make it in time.

Shortly before reaching the hospital, to our surprise, Rumer began to come to. Breathing better, eyes focusing, she sat up to pant as we pulled into the hospital parking lot, even beginning to "complain" about being there.

"Do you think we can just leave?" I asked Cheryl with hope in my heart that she'd think Rumer was well enough to take home.

"Well, while we're here, we should still have a doctor look at her," Cheryl told me. Seeing my disappointment, she added with relief beyond measure, "She really looks okay. I just think we should make sure."

I reluctantly dragged Rumer into the hospital, murmuring consolingly to her, her brown eyes pleading to leave each time they met mine. As we waited in the emergency room, one of the doctors came out to speak to us and to examine Rumer. She gave Rumer a quick check-up, looking closely at her gums and eyes, listening to her heart, and finally told us that she seemed to be fine. We were so grateful!

We quickly started back home. We were weak with relief and in tears with gratitude for our Rumer. She was still alive, okay, and coming home! Of course, she sat in Cheryl's lap in the passenger seat the whole way, going back and forth between sloppily kissing Cheryl and me as much as she could to anxiously staring through the windshield until the familiar sight of our property and home came into view. Many years later, our vet found that Rumer had a heart murmur. We always attributed it to this bee sting.

Whenever Cheryl and I encountered an unfortunate incident that forced us to take Rumer to an emergency vet appointment, we were always so afraid that her breed would pose a problem. We heard horror stories about what vet offices in Springfield made people with pit bulls do, the least being to make people muzzle their dogs before they even looked at them. We were also afraid that, because of her breed, the technicians or vets would treat her differently, uncaringly. We were very sensitive to this and extremely protective of Rumer, like a parent of her child. We refused to leave her with anyone. The one time we had to allow a vet take her into a back room to stitch a wound, we waited anxiously for her return, arguing about which one of us was going to barge into the room if she wasn't returned quickly. Because of all this, we were so worried to tell the truth. We always told vet offices that she was a "mix" breed.

It was only because Cheryl and I loved her so much and were so protective of her that we did this. While it is such a grave disservice to her and this beautiful breed, Cheryl and I experience daily the very fine line between living truthfully yet dangerously, and living a lie to be safe yet forfeiting your essence. We continued to hide Rumer's true identity. But in doing so, we inadvertently caused more harm for the breed despite all our good intentions.

It was a few years later that I was struck to the core when I read a few sentences on Diane Jessup's website one day. Ms. Jessup is a pit bull advocate who has written books, has a website, and is responsible for helping found the wonderful organization called Law Dogs, USA. I was doing research on the breed one day and came across her website where she stated that, in order to further help pit bulls get their good name back, it is important for responsible owners to proudly register them at their Town and City Halls as American Staffordshire Terriers.

This hit so deeply that we have since followed Ms. Jessup's advice with the two pit bulls we presently have. In desiring to change people's opinions and views on pit bulls every day of my life, it only makes sense that people know the positives, see my two wonderful representatives of the breed, and know what they are. At the same time, I cannot fault us for having hidden Rumer's true identity. Not many people realize the horror of the possibility of having one's dogs forcefully taken away and euthanized just because of their breed. I cannot even fathom this scenario when my dogs' only desire is to love and to be loved.

Life with Rumer was different, though. We were all different then. We never took her off the property, except when necessary, and she never wanted to leave. Thus was the start of a very unique and beautiful life together: Cheryl and me, my whole family, Rumer, and all our animals.

MIDDLE

There's so much truth to the saying:
If you love something, set it free.
If it comes back to you it's yours, if it doesn't it was never meant to be.

Nothing proved this truth more than my life with Rumer. I loved her more than anything, more than my life itself, but knew that many things made her happy besides me. Oh, I know she loved Cheryl and me in a special way, a reserved love that children only feel for mothers. Yet, she also loved my whole family, maybe differently, but no less.

Rumer loved my family so much that, I admit, I was somewhat jealous at first. It upset me to think that she might prefer to be with them more than Cheryl and me. It was a huge issue for me to overcome, this jealousy and fear and worry. I was consumed with it, so deep was her love for them. She never belonged to one person, or even to the two of us, like a lot of protective or sporting breed dogs. She chose the life that she wanted and what she wanted was all of us. Rumer made the choice herself to live at my parents' house during the day, yet, would always come back home at night to me and Cheryl. I can't deny how hard it was, but this was what made her life better, happier, more whole in a way that it wouldn't have been with just Cheryl and me alone. And, because of this, because of her, I began the journey of growth, of seeing and feeling and accepting that whatever made Rumer happy made me happy. It was a journey of learning the true meaning of "love."

As I traversed it, my immeasurable love for this soul allowed my jealousy and fear simply to be replaced with great appreciation and joy of my family's love for her. This, in turn, freed her not to have to choose or prefer anyone. She preferred us *all*. So, I continued, my growth beyond jealousy and fear bringing me to love her purely and without condition. And, because both I and my whole family loved her like this, she came back to each of us over and over. We allowed her spirit to be free and her life to be the most full, most unbelievable life I think a dog ever lived, enabling her to give the gift she had within her to all of us, unconditionally. All she wanted was the simplest of desires: love. And she gave herself, body and soul.

Ultimately, she taught me a most important lesson in life: to let go, whether of my fear, my selfishness, my need of "ownership," my worry, even *her*. I learned and finally understood that love isn't holding onto something, grasping it tightly in order to prevent it from escaping. Instead, love is being strong enough, safe enough, free enough to let it go, to allow one to live and love as they wish, as makes them happiest. She taught me that love is freedom, and instead of holding onto her, I filled myself up completely with my love for her and her love for me. I received so much more in return.

How so little we had to give, how so very much we gained. How lucky we all are to have been blessed with this little angel.

CHAPTER 27

Rumer's choice and desire to be a part of my whole family marked the start of a daily routine that continued for nine years. This routine varied slightly, depending on extenuating circumstances, but for the most part, stayed the same. She was free to roam back and forth between the two houses and the barn, enjoying the pond and the large field that separated our house from my parents'. She was never left outside unattended and loved to rotate among us, keeping my father company, sleeping on a chaise lounge with my mother or helping her prune the flowers, playing with Rob, watering the garden with Diane or Lee, or swimming or fixing equipment with Paul. She was everyone's best buddy, confidently a part of all we did. She was truly shared by everyone, intentionally designing her own life this way with foresight and perception that was, in retrospect, uncanny.

How smart she was, setting us all up so that everything benefited her life so perfectly. Soon after my family moved in, she initiated her plan. She knew that Cheryl and I had to go to work during the day. Wishing to be with one of us every minute of her life, Rumer knew that her odds for constant company were better at my parents' house. Since we made her the center of our universe, raising her from a puppy to be part of everything we did, she lived her life as if this was only natural.

Every morning, Rumer still began her day with me. Instead of our morning walks, we now had barn duty. Second only to a lush, green meadow mottled by the purple of waving clover buds, the barn with its smell of sweet hay and even sweeter horse has always been one of my favorite places. Opening the barn doors to this wonderful aroma,

79

Rumer and I fed the horses first. As I cleaned the stalls, changed water, and fetched hay, Rumer eventually branched out to the yard around the barn, sniffing and checking out all the new smells from overnight like when she was a baby. I glanced out of the barn often, keeping an eye on what she was doing, chuckling to myself at seeing her walking around so full of herself but looking so cute wearing a pink sweatshirt of mine on the cool mornings.

She checked back with me occasionally, biding her time, weighing what Cheryl and I had planned, trying to determine the best moment to make her way to Grammie's. At first, she thought I might try to stop her from leaving me, so she did it sneakily. Eventually, she brazenly made her way to Grammie's as if it were the only right thing to do.

Every once in a while, as Rumer meandered across the fields smelling for those unmentionables in which to roll, she looked back at me. Sometimes, she was so far from me and so close to my parents' house that all I saw was a vanilla speck with a black muzzle turned my way. I always yelled to her, "I love you Rumer!" This, in some way, freed her and allowed her to continue her pilgrimage.

There was almost always someone at the door to greet her when she arrived. I sometimes stopped my chores to curiously watch the whole process as Rumer arrived at my parents' house, able to see her back end and wagging tail, the rest of her hidden in the doorway as she looked in their side window. Her tail disappeared from my sight as the door opened, allowing her in. On those rare occasions when no one saw her waiting, her back end was visible to me for a few minutes, wagging and waiting good-naturedly, but, never very patient, she used her incredibly loud barking ploy, at which I could only laugh. The longer she had to wait, the more demanding her bark became until it was an emphatic demand, almost a yell of incredulity, "How dare they make me wait?!"

As the years went by, Rumer made her way to my parents' every weekday morning and stayed there all day, coming home at night to have her snacks and go to sleep with Cheryl and me. Rumer attained what she wanted: someone's attention at all times. She so casually orchestrated all that we did in order to accommodate that one need of hers. We, of course, weren't naïve to this; we just wanted the same thing and so were willing participants of such manipulation. What a completely fulfilling life she had going.

As much as Rumer loved staying at my parent's during the day, I was always so thankful that she loved coming home at night. It would have broken my heart otherwise, and maybe she knew that. I loved my routine with my Rumer and needed to have her body in bed, to hug, to hold, to love. Every evening, she "told" my family that she was ready to go back home by acting antsy. She went to the front door, turned, and stared at everyone in the living room. If my family didn't react quickly enough, she initiated the famous sideways stare, curling her mouth up into a smile, voicing her irritating "harrrrr" ("I want to leave *now*").

Most evenings, Lee and Diane brought her back home through the fields, playing along the way, running and chasing Rumer's tail as she laughed and ducked, or, tucking her butt and taking off, running past their playful grabs. If it was very cold, they drove her home right to the back door or front sidewalk. They lifted her out of the car saying, "Go tell your Mommies you're home, Rumer." Laughing, walking in her slinky way, she barked to announce herself. Before they left, Lee and Diane always waited to make sure she was let in safely.

The fun continued once Rumer made it home every evening. Cheryl and I loved settling into bed at night, our whole family back together. It was "bed and snacks" and up the stairs we trotted, Rumer excitedly bounding up ahead of us. She reached the bedroom, tore down the carpet runner, and made a flying leap onto the bed to get her pile of snacks on a little placemat. Her "snacks" consisted of a few dog cookies with an occasional box of raisins. She saved the raisins for last, methodically ripping the box apart, placing the pieces to the side in order to get to the sweets inside. She chewed each raisin so carefully, savoring the juicy morsels. Most of her other "snacks" consisted of her multivitamin, other supplements, and later, her pain medications.

On special nights, Cheryl or I looked forward to giving her a "dolly," a favorite dog toy from Wal-Mart that was stuffed and had rope arms and legs. I begged Cheryl to let me be the one to get it for her since it made me so happy to see her excitement. On my way back downstairs to the cabinet in which we kept a bag full of these toys, I walked by her, my hand trailing along her body, and told her, "Rumer, stay here, I have a special treat for you."

She waited on the bed while I went, intently watching the stair landing, ears perked, head cocked. When I returned, hiding it behind my back, she quivered and jumped with excitement. Once in front of her, I pulled out "dolly," this simple toy making her so happy. She took it from me with great joy and spent the rest of the night working at that "dolly." Nibbling with her front teeth, she always started by making a small hole. From this hole, she pulled out all the stuffing piece by piece and spit it out to the side, going faster and faster as she went, head flicking back and forth in fast motion. I had horrible flashbacks to Lambie as she did this, the end product suspiciously like that of Lambie's untimely demise. After sufficiently destroying Dolly, she collapsed on her side and fell into the peaceful, happy, exhausted sleep of a job well done.

I love to read for hours into the night, the TV and lights on low, everyone sleeping but me. It is a source of great comfort and I look forward to this time all day long. Each night before I succumbed to sleep there was one last act I performed. Getting up, I went to Rumer and touched her lightly so as not to startle her. Picking her head up in my hands, looking into her sleepy brown eyes, kissing the top of her head right in the middle of that deep ridge, I said to her, "I love thee so, Angel Pie." Quoting from Elizabeth Barrett Browning I said with all the love in my heart, "How do I love thee, let me count the ways." As I looked into her squinting gaze, I just couldn't imagine how there could be more love anywhere in the world than what was in my heart for her.

Then, as she slept so soundly and peacefully, she dreamed. Even her dreams were full of fun and activity, her legs running in her sleep, her muffled "woofing" at something she was chasing in her mind. She often woke us with all of this dream activity and the drumming of her paws on our sleeping bodies. Her tail thumped heavily and steadily as she loved even in her dreams.

Strong girl, so muscular and warm, breathing so softly in your sleep, putting me at peace. How I love to cuddle and spoon your beautiful young body, kissing your head when I wake occasionally through the night, right between where your ears slope toward your eyes, that muscular bulge. You smell like baked pork—I could eat you up. I smell you with love, I hold you with reverence.

CHAPTER 28

Throughout the years, Rumer became such an integral part of everything we did. She helped plant Douglas, a Douglas fir, in front of the barn, ripping and dragging the burlap sack in which the roots sat and then helping drag it to the hole. She monitored all other plantings, from flowers to vegetables. We used her in photographs to gage how much something we planted had grown. She even helped to husk corn, taking each ear and methodically ripping the green leaves carefully, spitting out the fuzz at the top of the ears in a glorious frenzy.

When she wasn't helping with chores, she was seen riding the property with Lee on the Honda ATV, Rumer sitting on the seat in front, oftentimes wearing sunglasses, laughing as the wind rushed by them. As Rumer became older and got bigger, she loved riding the golf cart, the Number 8, instead of the ATV. The golf cart was *perfect*. She "uppied" to lounge on the front seat and watch everyone's activities at her leisure.

We understood so well all of those vintage photographs of families with their pit bulls. They always seemed to be so much a part of these families, doing human things, most of the time a child's arm around them, the "nursemaids" for which they were so nicknamed. So, when Rumer did do "doggie" things, like rolling in deer or goose poop, it surprised us greatly. But oh did she love finding the right ripe pile of green poop in the fields as she made her way around the property, her nose pulling her toward such beacons of bliss. It was really the only thing she did that reminded us of her "dogness."

Every time she found and perfumed herself with these unmentionables, the lucky one she approached first screamed with disgust. An emergency bath obviously followed. This gross habit resulted in green, smelly smears of slime all over her face, ears, and shoulders. It was completely repulsive in look, feel, and smell. It was really the only thing she did that made any of us angry with her. She, however, thought it was the best thing ever. She approached us, moseying in the way that defined her, like a Slinky going side to side, laughing and wagging her tail in pleasure. She was so happy with herself and her new smell. Many times, I found that I had to carry her into the house and up into the shower, stripping myself, and showering both of us clean.

One brutally cold mid-winter day, Rumer oh-so-happily came to me in this awful condition. I was home alone that morning, finishing up at the barn and getting ready to go in to start preparing for work. When I saw Rumer approach, I noticed the green, horrible-smelling slime covering her head and neck and was so repulsed I couldn't even find it in me to bring her in the house. She was just too dirty and smelly, having slimed herself extra well.

I quickly decided to take the barn hose and try to clean her outside, something about which I still feel terribly guilty. The water coming out the hose was ice cold, as was the air. When this ice water hit her head, she dropped to the ground as if shot, moaning a cry I never heard from her before or since. I immediately stopped, horrified at myself for what I had just done. Then, I found myself coming to the horrible realization that, with Rumer already wet and leaking green slimy smelly poop, I had to take her inside to finish cleaning and bathing her. To add insult to injury, Rumer decided to shake herself as I stood there frozen in indecision, green poop flying everywhere, including all over me.

After all was said and done, I admitted my sin to my family and Cheryl, feeling so guilty about it that I couldn't keep it to myself. Thus was born one of her many nicknames: "Rumie Frozen Brains." This was one of which I wasn't very proud!

Aside from the smell and unhygienic reasons, the deer and goose poop also caused Rumer to have numerous bouts with giardia. Each time the giardia resurfaced, she needed to begin a course of antibiotics since it caused greenish, explosive diarrhea. Unfortunately, this happened almost every spring.

CHAPTER 29

Cheryl and I found that Rumer developed a deep and all-consuming love for any activity that challenged her and tested her "gameness." In all the books we bought and read and all the research that Cheryl and I did on pit bulls, the word "springpole" kept appearing. Springpoles are, in essence, rope hung from springs (for give) so that a dog can jump up, grab the rope with their teeth, and hang. All the information we read claimed that pit bulls love to do this, and love nothing more. We found out first-hand how true this is.

That summer, Cheryl and I purchased a thick, soft rope and attached it to a heavy spring. We then tied the spring to a nice branch on the tree outside our back door, the branch having the perfect angle and height. As soon as we put it up, it immediately became Rumer's favorite activity. She loved her springpole so much that it quickly became an obsession. Jumping and grabbing the rope at the highest possible point, she swung back and forth in mid-air, body thrashing side to side as she shook it. She easily did this for hours and became very sore, so we soon found that we had to limit her time. We had to take the rope away from her and loop it back over the tree branch so she couldn't reach it. She became a permanent fixture under the tree and sat there for hours, staring up at her rope, barking and whining for someone to let her have it. And, when someone finally did come with a long stick or the pool skimmer pole to get the rope down for her, she went crazy with excitement.

One beautiful summer day, the leaves of the Poplar trees rustling musically in the slight breeze, Paul's girlfriend Katie came to visit, bringing her mother and her niece. Rumer had a particular joke that she liked to play on Katie. She loved to surprise her by jumping straight up in the air, licking her face, and touching back down, never laying a paw on her, panting and laughing at her accomplishment. She knew that Katie didn't really appreciate this and, like with Monnie, teased Katie over and over with this joke.

What Katie did appreciate, however, was Rumer's springpole prowess. She was so impressed that she asked us if we would let Rumer hang on her rope for her mother and niece to see. Rumer put on an extra special show that day as she whipped the rope back and forth, showing off her beautiful, strong body. Katie's mother and niece couldn't believe it; they never saw anything like it. They clapped and applauded and laughed at everything Rumer showed them.

This one small joy in Rumer's life made a huge impression on them, especially on Katie's mother. Katie told us many years later, when her mother was in a nursing home with Alzheimer's, that it was one of the few things her mother could recall. Even though she couldn't always remember her own children, she remembered Rumer and would say, "That dog. Can you believe it? Hanging from a tree like that?!"

Another fetish of Rumer's was chasing and chewing on rocks. Unlike the springpole, this was one I should have discouraged. I can't understand why I allowed this and, once again a negligent mother, I threw her beloved rock one day as she was harassing me to no end. I was busy with some barn chore that had to be finished, so threw it without really paying attention. She didn't mind. She eagerly chased it and brought it back to me happily, pleased with herself for such a great fetch.

As I glanced at her, I did a slight double-take. Was that *blood* that I could see running down her chin and neck? In a panic, I grabbed her, made her drop the stone, and pried her mouth open. She was so good about letting us do anything to her, whether it was looking in her mouth or poking and prodding her wherever we needed to. To my horror, I found that one of her front bottom teeth had been knocked out by the bounce of the stone. Her beautiful white, perfect teeth! Completely my fault, I was sickened by what I did. Rumer didn't seem to mind and she didn't seem hurt, but I was so upset that I had again marred her perfect body.

From that point on, I refused to let Rumer play with rocks. We all reprimanded her and ignored her pleas. We changed her focus and bought tennis balls for her, which thankfully did the trick. She loved tennis balls so much that they became an almost permanent fixture in her mouth, her new obsession.

I was even more grateful for this soon after, when we had to take her springpole away for good, too. After playing on her springpole one day, Rumer came in the house to rest and cool off from the heat of the summer afternoon. Cheryl and I ate lunch as Rumer lay on the cool tile floor, panting happily. While she lay there, I began to notice blood dripping off her tongue and onto the light tiles. Thinking that she just might have bitten her tongue, we checked her mouth to find, again to my horror, another missing tooth next to the one that was already gone. Due to the missing bottom tooth, the teeth on each side of the missing one were now in a vulnerable state and easily knocked out.

That did it. We immediately took down Rumer's springpole, sadly. In retrospect, it was somewhat fortuitous since she developed arthritis at a very young age only a few years later. With the arthritis, she couldn't afford any added soreness.

CHAPTER 30

It's almost dusk on a peaceful summer evening, cooling after a hot day, as I sit by the pool. I hear my father's hearty laugh, Paul's clapping hands intermingled with the sound, echo across the fields from their house out back…a laugh that I *know* Rumer has somehow provoked. With the fading of this wonderful laugh, I find myself reflecting on what Rumer has meant to all of us. Each of us developed our own special relationship with Rumer that we cherished, our own special time with her. With the relaxing, late afternoon sounds in the background, my eyelids began to get heavy as I thought…

Rumer's and Paul's relationship reminded me so much of brother and sister. Paul, so much like a dog himself that we nicknamed him "coy boy," and Rumer so much like a person, they met perfectly in the middle as long-lost siblings.

My parents' basement is a wonderful place to spend time. It is a large, clean, cemented area, making it ideal for Rumer to play in no matter what time of year. Paul keeps a collection of hockey sticks here and found out quickly that hockey became one of Rumer's favorite games. He began to keep tennis balls on the edge of the basement window, hockey sticks lined up underneath in waiting. Lounging in my parents' living room, they suddenly looked at each other.

"Do you wannah go play?" (eventually, this just became, "D.") Paul asked her, barely able to get it out of his mouth before Rumer started yelling in happiness, scraping and scratching across the floor in her haste to get to the basement door. Her "basement play" yell was like no other. It was a screaming yell of greatest delight as they raced each other down to the basement, boy and dog.

What was so great about this game? Why all the excitement? And, what did it involve that caused us all to hear their play from above, a great racket of yelling and clapping and things getting thrown about? I needed to see, so I followed one Sunday after our dinner, waiting to see what all the fuss was, standing well out of harm's way from these two maniacs.

As soon as they made it to the basement, Rumer ran to the window ledge for her tennis ball. She couldn't *wait* to have Paul flip one of the balls to her. She held this ball in her mouth while Paul put another tennis ball on the floor. Then they were off, Paul running around the cellar with his hockey stick, moving the ball around while Rumer ran after him, trying to block.

Rumer continuously voiced her "Rrrrr" sound, hopping on her front legs, all pumped up in excitement, shaking her head from side to side as Paul shot the ball. Most of the time, she blocked his shots, so much spittle flying as she shook her head that the basement floor was covered with her saliva.

Paul taught her that he was "winning" when he got by her, or got a shot past her, clapping and yelling in victory with a loud, "Yahoooo." She couldn't stand this! She flung herself with abandon after that ball, screeching and scraping on the cement floor around corners, avoiding all the exercise equipment with great precision, in order to get that ball and stop Paul. Their play was so rough, but that's how she loved it! They checked each other, bounced off of each other, pushed, tripped, and every other dirty trick. Paul couldn't believe how she knew the game and what a good player she was.

And, it was Paul who loved to torture Rumer with the threat of a bath. Every time Paul took a shower, he got his towel, went into the living room, and looked at Rumer, who was lying on the couch or living room rug. She saw his towel and gave him her sideways look.

"Rumer, do you want a bath?" Paul teased.

This was so hateful to Rumer that she yelled at Paul and got up, prepared to run. Paul chased her as she took off, barking over her shoulder, again scraping and sliding around the corners of my parents' tiled floors like a cartoon character. He finally stopped chasing her and started laughing while saying, "Okay, just teasing Rumie." This was her invitation to walk slowly to him, head down, slinking along, wagging her tail and laughing, still not totally trusting of his intentions. And, sometimes she was right not to trust, for when she got close, Paul started the whole process over, grabbing at her tail as she took off once again.

Come summertime, as sunlight shimmered off the gentle ripples in the pool, periodically blinding me, I sat poolside watching Rumer and Paul. Not the normal dog, Rumer *asked* to go swimming when she wanted to cool off on a hot afternoon or evening. It was usually Paul who took her. I watched them, an occasional flycatcher swooping down gracefully to grab an unfortunate bug from the top of the water. Rumer showed her desire by approaching the side of the pool in request and Paul, in the pool, said, "Do you want to come swimming, Rumie?" If her answer was "yes," she walked up to him and shyly placed her paw on his shoulder. Paul, scooping her butt under one arm, placed his other around her back. She let him take her into the water this way, holding her like a baby, cheek pressed against Paul's cheek, eyes closed in trust. He bobbed around the pool, holding her like this, going under up to their necks to cool off.

In such opposition to the sweetness of their swims, it seemed as though Paul was meant to be Rumer's tormentor. One of his favorite tortures, he hung over his balcony on the second floor of my parents' house yelling, "Yehah!!" Rumer heard this from inside our house and went crazy. Cheryl or I had to hurriedly let her out and, in her excitement and haste, she *flew* off our back deck to my parents' through the fields, over the brooks, and up their hill at warp speed. Paul got the same effect if he just stood in my parents' driveway and threw a tennis ball up and down in his hands for Rumer to see wherever she was on the property. A possible game she was missing out on? No way!

Oh, the smell of frying beef kidney. Not the most pleasant of smells to us, but to Rumer?... Superb! Rob was Rumer's gourmet chef. Since she lived most days at my parents' house, Rob loved to shop for her and loved to cook everything she ate, including the wonderful beef kidney, chicken, potatoes, or whatever everyone else ate for dinner that night. He made sure she ate very healthy and wholesome foods.

Though he was Rumer's chef, Rob also loved playing with her. She was such a fun play buddy since she understood every game and never gave up. "Thump... thump... thump." From the living room, Cheryl and I heard the sound of a tennis ball bouncing down our roof as Rob and Rumer played "Roof Ball." A favorite game of Rumer's, Rob threw her ball up onto the house or barn roof over and over for her. As it came bouncing down, Rumer shook with excitement and waited for it to bounce at the perfect height in order to jump and catch it in mid-air.

Since Rumer loved doing all kinds of acrobatics in order to catch her balls, Rob later got the idea to buy a baseball net for her. "Net Ball" really tested her athletic ability since, after being thrown at the net, the ball came back at her fast and she couldn't tell which way it would go. She was the quickest and most coordinated mover I ever saw.

In the winter, they played "Snow Ball." Rob got busy making a dozen or so snowballs and lined them up in preparation. I watched out the kitchen window as Rumer waited, barking relentlessly, yelling at him to hurry. When Rob finished, he flung them side to side, his arm a blur, Rumer running back and forth to catch them. And, Rumer *did* catch most of them, so fast herself, flattening out all the snow in her path with effort. For those few she didn't catch, she spent the rest of her time searching every square inch of the area, finding the wayward snowballs to dig them apart or pick them up to shake them into pieces. We eventually had to limit "Snow Ball" since it caused Rumer to become incontinent at times.

Rob loved doing everything with Rumer. He couldn't believe how intuitive and intelligent she was, how knowing she was, how fun she was. He often said that Rumer was the best friend he ever had in his whole life.

"Ouch!"

It inevitably happened. Considering all the rough play that Rumer liked, she sometimes couldn't help but catch someone's finger or scratch one of us. When this happened, she became very upset if someone got hurt. She actually understood what the word "hurt" meant and immediately stopped her play to start licking apologetically. She might not even have been the offender, but if she heard the words "hurt" or "ouch!" she stopped playing to apologize. She was so sensitive that it sometimes took a lot of cajoling to get her to play again. Sometimes, she couldn't even be enticed into playing anymore, so sad to have hurt one of us. Unbelievably, we even had to start being careful of saying the word "hurt" in her presence if we didn't want her to be sad the rest of the day.

It was a beautiful sight and one that I will never forget: two girls, one brunette, one vanilla, riding the golf cart at top speed, the wind whipping one's hair and the other's tongue. Diane and Rumer, best buddies. The two of them traversed the property, watering plants, riding the golf cart, the Number 8, Rumer adorned with baseball cap and sunglasses, laughing in the wind.

Diane worried to an obsessive degree about Rumer getting hurt on her watch and often warned her, "Rumer, you stay on this cart. Do not jump off—I'll be right back," as she went to the brook to draw water for the plants. But, Rumer loved to tease Diane. As soon as Diane started down the few stairs that my father had built to the scenic front brook, Rumer flew off the cart and ran after something made-up. This gave Diane a heart attack!

"I warned you, Rumer...Let's go!" she said as she led Rumer back into the house in order to reflect on her disobedience.

Rumer trudged, in her slinky fashion, after Diane up the walkway to the house, head down in shame but eyes aglitter with mischief, tongue out in full laughter, walking in super-slow motion because she knew she was being punished. After a short amount of time, Diane, unable to be without her for long, let Rumer out once again to enjoy the rest of the day.

Funny dog, pulling such stunts to be our clown, laughing and laughing, taking your momentary solitary confinement in order to play a joke on someone or humor us in any way...

Diane loved playing ball games with Rumer too, and together with Lee played her favorite—hockey in the basement—when Paul couldn't. In Rumer's last year, Diane became her primary caretaker. It so happened that Diane lost her job that year and began to work part-time. This enabled her to be home to care for Rumer. By that time, Rumer needed someone with her almost every minute and I really don't know how long we could have held on to her without Diane adjusting her schedule to do this. To that end, I will be forever grateful.

Immortalized on film is Lee's "No!" and pointed finger at baby Rumer, with a bratty little bark and budding sideways glance being Rumer's rebellious reply. This playful teasing back and forth started very early, when Rumer was just a few months old, but they already understood each other so well. The two of them had a very special connection that I don't believe can ever be duplicated. From puppyhood on, Lee treated Rumer as a sister, an equal, practically teaching Rumer how to behave as a person. You could have a conversation with Rumer and know she understood, mainly because of Lee. She taught Rumer almost everything from language to posing for pictures to riding all the toys—the ATV, golf cart, tractor...making Rumer a part of everything.

Rumer loved to accompany Lee everywhere on the property. She watched Lee with a human-like concentration and knew Lee's every thought and intention. Each morning, after she made her way up to Grammie's, Rumer began her day in Lee's room. Jumping on Lee's bed, she studied her intently, trying to determine if this was a work day or play day. If Lee started to put on her work clothes, Rumer got very upset. Lee had to tell her, "Rumer, I have to go to work, but you'll have a good day with everyone else. I'll come home fast, okay?" Rumer couldn't stand this. Turning dejectedly and jumping off the bed, she left Lee's room, not wanting to face a goodbye.

Sometimes, on a day off, Lee dressed in her shopping clothes. Rumer knew the difference and didn't get upset with this—she knew her Auntie Lee would only be gone a short while. Lee took Rumer's head, kissed the top of it, and told her, "Pie Pie, I'm just going out for a while but I'll be right back." And Rumer waited, by the window or out in the driveway or poking around the yard for juicy unmentionables, listening for the slightest sound of Lee's car returning to her, tires crunching up the gravel drive.

Rumer and Lee were undoubtedly very connected, not even needing words to communicate. These two understood each other their whole lives on a much deeper level. Rumer also revealed her complete love and trust in Lee by the buttered pieces of toast she left hiding under Lee's pillow! After searching the whole house with her treasured toast, she found there was just no safer place.

Grammie's laughter and exclamation of, "Oh, Rumer! You still think you're a little baby!" were often heard whenever Rumer struggled, even as an adult, to share Grammie's recliner for a nap. When Rumer was little, sharing this chair was her favorite thing to do with her Grammie and posed no problem. But, as Rumer grew, she didn't realize that she wasn't a little baby anymore that could fit places so easily. Wanting to lie with Grammie in "their" chair, she gamely struggled to climb up with her. Getting stuck, her front feet on the chair, scrambling, trying to get her back feet up one at a time, so gently but still heavy and so accidentally hurting Grammie, a lot of commotion ensued, the chair rocking back and forth wildly in protest. Rumer eventually turned around to face out, and lay down in between Grammie's legs with a big sigh and blow of her cheeks. Grammie was exhausted and Rumer was laughing and panting with the effort, but both so happy at the accomplishment. Occasionally, the chair tried to snap shut on both of them, causing Grammie to scream, the chair to squeak and snap, and Rumer to laugh through it all, thinking she caused the funniest things to happen.

Eyes in a squint, jaws slowly chewing side to side, Rumer loved chewing gum. It was Grammie's job to start a piece for her and chew it to just the right consistency. Rumer, sitting in front of her, watching intently, waited patiently for Grammie to get the gum ready and blow a bubble to just the right size. As Grammie blew the bubble and leaned forward, Rumer leaned in to meet Grammie, taking the bubble from her lips so gently. She never grabbed at it or touched Grammie, always so careful. She then chewed the gum for a very long time, tongue coming out and rolling with every chew, the sides of her lips raised with the effort.

"Come on, Rumer, let's go find some nice trees," said Grammie with a smile. Rumer, cocking her head, ears perked to this request, followed Grammie to the golf cart, leapt up, and lounged on the seat as Grammie started driving. The sound of the electric golf cart, the sweet jingling of the hanging chimes bouncing along in its basket, revealed Grammie's place on the property as she and Rumer rode around, Grammie's hand lovingly placed on her Rumer as Rumer's head swiveled this way and that. They rode around the whole property, Rumer helping Grammie scope out the perfect tree branches on which to hang Grammie's cherished wind chimes. Rumer loved watching Grammie do this, hopping off the cart at each stop to help. Thank goodness for Grammie's obsession. We are fortunate to have so many wind chimes around the property that even a slight breeze will cause beautiful and varied tones, from high bells to bamboo clonking. It is wonderful indeed.

In with the brilliant reds and golds of fall came the wonderful bounty of delicious nuts from the trees that grew along the front of our property. Grammie and Rumer, riding their cart in search of these fresh nuts, found them on the ground by the hundreds. Together, they sat to enjoy sharing this natural treat. Grammie, gathering as many as she could fit in her sunhat, sat on a boulder and cracked open the shells to get to the sweet meat inside. Rumer loved this nut meat and sat patiently in front of Grammie, eyes squinting in concentration, as she watched this process, waiting for her pieces. Grammie never disappointed, loving her Rumer so much that she shared this hard-earned nut meat with her granddaughter.

"I'm her last choice. She only comes to me when no one else is home," my father always said. But, that wasn't necessarily true. One of Rumer's favorite things was to share Papa's toast and coffee in the mornings (probably the same toast that Lee would later feel under her pillow). And, when everyone else *was* gone, she was a great buddy to him. She loved to keep him company in the house, on the couch with him for a morning nap, and outside, helping him with projects he had undertaken in the yard and supervising them to make sure Papa did everything properly.

When it came to the person Rumer trusted most, no one could argue that it was Cheryl. Her trust in Cheryl was as implicit and complete as one could feel for a mother. Cheryl was her nurse and her healer, Cheryl's hands soothing and comforting, always able to help with whatever might be wrong. Rumer looked to Cheryl when she needed relief from pain, when she needed to understand why something wasn't right, or when she needed healing, both body and soul.

Lazy summer vacation afternoons or weekend days brought deep-summer stillness, ceiling fan whirring, circulating a much-needed breeze, and sounds of neighborhood kids' yells or dirt bikes in the distance. Cheryl and Rumer lay in a cool comfortable bed for a nap, shades drawn to the sun, the room slightly illuminated with the muted relaxing rays of sunlight. Rumer loved, as much as anything else in life, to see Cheryl making the climb up our stairs in the afternoons to the bedroom for a nap.

Some afternoons, Rumer was outside helping me. Tired and sweaty from my chores, I looked at her to say, "Come on, Ru. Let's take a break." She followed me in the house, unaware that Cheryl might be upstairs napping. "Rumer, Mommy's upstairs in bed," I told her. I know without a doubt that animals have emotions. I saw it then, in Rumer, the joy in her face as I said this. Her head flicked to the stairway, cocked to the side, ears perked, hoping she heard me correctly. When she looked back at me, I nodded and said, "Go ahead. Mommy's in bed," and she bounded up the stairs to settle in with Cheryl. Making a nest next to her mother, she turned and scratched at the blankets, flopping down on them heavily, grunting and sighing in total contentment.

My grandmother, Ma, always held a large, special part in our lives. She was our caretaker when we were young children and a second mother to us all. "Look at that little bulldog," she exclaimed with a smile when she first laid eyes on baby Rumer. Ma was over 90-years-old and living in a nursing home when Rumer was a baby. We visited her there, Cheryl and I taking Rumer to see her, and Ma loved this, as did some of the other residents. Most of the time, though, someone in my family picked Ma up at the nursing home and brought her to my parents' house for dinner.

During these visits, Ma and Rumer developed a very close, funny relationship revolving around food. My mother has a beautiful, long dining room table at which we can all fit for Sunday and holiday dinners. She decorates it stunningly, even Martha Stewart would be proud, for these occasions. When we all sat down to eat, we noticed something very suspicious. Rumer started to sit under the table at Ma's knees. I, who sat next to Ma, lifted the tablecloth and bent down a little to see what Rumer was doing. I could see her just sitting there, head on Ma's lap, eyes just visible and staring intently up at Ma through the crack between the tablecloth and Ma's knees. Curiosity over Rumer's choice of place got the best of us and we began to look for a reason.

What first tipped us off were the red sauce stains that appeared on Ma's lap. In the Italian tradition, we almost always had homemade pasta with our meals. After noticing these sauce stains, we watched more intently. Sure enough, we saw...

Ma, when she suspected no one was looking, quickly snuck food down onto her lap. Rumer, in the ready position, gulped it down as quickly as it was placed there. If Ma suspected anyone was watching,

she yelled, surprisingly loudly, at Rumer, "Now, get out of here—GET
OUT!" as if Rumer was bothering her and sitting where she shouldn't.
While yelling at Rumer, she waved her hands in the air and dismissed
her adamantly, her lap covered in sauce and crumbs. Rumer obediently
got up from under the table and hunched away into the living room,
looking dejectedly back at Ma over her shoulder, playing the poor, sad
dog so perfectly. What a great act they had going!

Me, I thought… What was my special connection with Rumer?

I know I was responsible for a lot of the fun play with her, the loud
play, the obnoxious play. Cheryl's familiar, "Would you please quiet
down? I never knew two creatures louder than you!" followed us as we
teased each other, yelling and running around the house in fun. Cheryl
thought we were both crazy.

I also have to take the blame for Rumer's hatred of brushes. It really
started out as a fun game, but a game I took a little too far. Approaching
her with her nice soft brush, I asked her, "Can I brush you, Rumie?"

She knew I was asking this teasingly, so ran from me. I laughed
and chased her, trying to run the brush over her as we both ran around
the house, loud and chaotic, hoping no one was in our path. Rumer,
however, *really* developed a hatred for being brushed. Although a game
for the most part, if I tried to calm her down and nicely brush her, she
couldn't stand it. Along with so many other hygienic activities, this was
abandoned, Rumer never being brushed in her life. It's a good thing she
swam a lot and had many baths due to her rolling in unmentionables.

I did so many things with Rumer. She was my barn buddy, my
cuddle buddy, my play buddy. But, was I special to her? Sometimes I
don't know any more. I sometimes berate myself…did I take enough
time out of my busy day for her, did I play with her enough, feed her
enough, enjoy just relaxing with her enough, show her how much I
loved her enough? Was I a good enough mother? I hope I did and
was all of these things enough with Rumer, that I was a little bit of
everything to her. But, was I?

All I know is that I loved everything there was about Rumer. I
loved watching her, whether playing with the family, sniffing around
the yard, guarding the horses, or just sleeping—especially sleeping. I
loved that she was always a fixture in our picturesque landscape, loved
to look out at any time and see her familiar shape, out and about with

one of my family members or Cheryl, working, walking, watching, playing, or lounging. I loved seeing her grow, from that perfect pony-puppy to a skinny teenager to a splendid, strong, and perfect adult. I loved her sweetness, her funniness, her consideration, her strength, how giving she was, how knowledgeable she was, and the familiarity we had together. I loved her willingness to help everyone, whether with getting better from being sick, with all the property activities, or with helping prepare for our many family get-togethers. I loved how she looked, how she smelled, her gentle kisses, her greetings that never ever failed to meet me at the door. I loved how she felt when I hugged her, her crooked back toes, her profile, complete with moles, as she watched the yard. I loved her spirit that showed itself in that 5-week-old puppy's eyes and that continued to grow stronger as she did, becoming addicting to everyone exposed to it. Her spirit was pure, it was generous, it was wise, and it was free and, in being all of this, it couldn't help but make those of us around her smile, love, laugh, and enjoy life. And, I so loved and was so proud of being her mother for all of these reasons and many more. Did she know that I even loved the very fact of loving her?

As it happens, life was busy and we experienced many events as the years only too quickly passed. My best friend's suicide, family estrangements, new animals, problems at work… Rumer was the constant throughout everything, the unchanging, loving, unconditional rock that propelled everyone through everything. She always knew and was sensitive to when we were blue or in a sad mood. She went out of her way to comfort us, whether with soft kisses or her typical clownish behavior, to make us laugh or smile, not ever caring if it was at her own expense.

My Savior, my Teacher, my eternal clown, always happy, always laughing, always trying to make others as happy as you always are yourself. Your only condition…always being in the company of someone you love, never left alone. We are all your most treasured and beloved possessions. You are the one to whom we cry, who we hug or to whom we tell our troubles, your brown understanding eyes so grounding, so wise, our silent empath. You are always able to put all of our problems in perspective with your constant presence and unwavering strength. Oh, how we become complacent in the routine of our lives. I often wonder, where did all of my time with you go?

My perfect little puppy!   Sand up my nose makes me sneeze!

Shy girl, posing.   Quadding with Auntie Lee.

My Halloween pirate.

My mother's caption-
What more can be said?

Happy Birthday, Rumer!

Helping to husk the corn.

Super Bowl party

Parties make Rumer so happy—Especially Halloween.

Best Halloween outfit—
Uncle Paul's racecar!

Dressed up for July 4th.

Ma and Rumer in action. Did they really think we couldn't see?

Swimming—Rumer's style!

Helping Grammie open her Christmas gifts.

Uncle Paul and Rumer after a hard day of play.

Laughing in front of the barn amongst the beautiful flowers.

Auntie Lee and her greatest Love.

Their way of relaxing.

Sleeping with Taja.

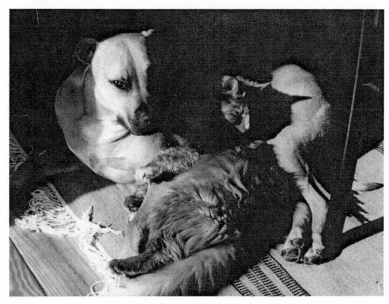

Cuddling with Monnie.

Ever watchful of that untrustworthy horse, Cesa.

Lily and Rumer—Best of friends.

Rumer's simplest
Halloween outfit.

Snowballs anyone?   Napping with Grammie.

Rumer's favorite activity with Uncle Paul, after hockey, of course.

Poolside

All the girls having fun: Cheryl,
Diane, Lee, Rumer, and me.

Loving Selena.

Jolene Mercadante

On the golf cart with Grammie staking out
the best place to hang wind chimes.

Last Christmas together, 2003: Rumer, Paul, Pops, Grammie,
me, Rob, Cheryl, Lee & Honey, Diane & Sweetie.

Grammie and Pops with their Love.

Swimming with the baby ducks.

 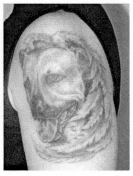

On the Number 8 sandwiched
by Diane and Lee.

My beautiful
tattoo.

Aderyn and Mei Mei, my two beautiful girls!

Chapter 31

Beautiful, strong girl, so willing to do what any of us want, as long as it involves doing it with you. I can still see you laughing, proudly posing for pictures, your missing bottom teeth, your black muzzle just beginning to turn white on your chin. I hope you know, there could be no greater love in this world than mine for you…

Rumer approached middle age with a great physical explosion. Where the teenage Rumer had been very thin and lanky, she suddenly looked more and more like her father, very muscular, stocky, and strong. Her body looked like the "typical" pit bull terrier, her head developing that ridge down the middle surrounded by muscular jaws, shedding the girlish body that our barn carpenter, Gerry, had so not believed belonged to a full pit bull. Her ears folded just right, picture perfect pit bull ears.

With Rumer's physical change came a great mental change. She enjoyed just relaxing with everyone, becoming a great "lap" dog—as much as a 75 pound dog could be a "lap" dog. She squished herself onto the couch, one careful paw at a time, always in between Cheryl and me, pushing and adjusting until she was comfortable. We, of course, were shuffled aside but were always willing to make room for her.

Rumer lounged by the pool in the summer with us, insisting on lying on a chaise lounge, most of the time with Grammie. She knew to be careful since the chaise lounge contains holes in the squared fabric, and avoided these holes with the grace of a ballet dancer, turning to lie in between Grammie's legs like on their recliner. She never wanted to use a towel on the deck anymore and, forget "doggie things" like Cooleroos and dog hammocks—she knew those were for dogs. Sometimes, she had her own lounge, the rest of us lying on the deck on a towel. But, as long as Rumer was comfortable and happy, that's all that mattered.

At my parents' house, she had her spot in the middle of the couch, forcing people to sit on each side of her. She surveyed the yard out of my parents' front bay window from here, attending her duties, able to see everything from animals crossing the yard to people pulling into the driveway.

I can't seem to remember how it started or who started it, but this is when Rumer began to eat only if she was fed with a fork. I'm sure it was another manipulation so subtly devised by Rumer that I'll never be able to remember. At mealtime, each of her home-cooked meals was placed in her bowl and brought to her on the living room rug at my parents' house. Rumer, lying down next to her bowl, glanced at her food and then looked at us. Her gaze wavered between her bowl and each of us, black eyebrows moving up and down as her eyes shifted, waiting patiently for someone to feed her. Sometimes we tried to out wait her, just to see what happened if we didn't feed her right away. Oh, she just kept lying there, a very patient girl, indeed, when it had to do with being fed properly. Patience only lasted so long, however, and if we waited too long, she gave us her sideways look and made her irritating "harrrrrrr" noise. This did it! One of my sisters, both of whom loved to feed her, always got down on the floor next to her and fed her with a fork. She was very good at eating this way and didn't miss a crumb.

Rumer ate every meal this way the rest of her life. When home, Cheryl and I had to feed her this way, too. She expected this and we loved her so much that we happily complied. It made it even easier when we knew Rumer so appreciated it. After every meal, she got up and thanked us for feeding her, showering us with messy, food-filled kisses every time and without fail.

Rumer also became employed at this time in her life. Granted, it was a self-appointed job, but in her esteem, an extremely important one. She believed it was her sole responsibility to keep our horses in their fence (the electric fence obviously not good enough). This was a two-fold blessing: it gave Rumer something to do besides being obsessed with her sticks and balls, and it gave us the opportunity to get some yard work done.

So familiar that it became the ordinary was Rumer, sitting at her post by the horse fence, tennis ball in mouth. Once in a while the horses walked around or, Heaven forbid, ran in play. Suddenly, Rumer was there, running along the fence with them. She was lightning fast when she was running full out. She kept pace with the horses from the outside, rounding the corners at full speed, her left back leg always the one spiraling to the outside. As they stopped to eat or nap, she sat and stared at them, not even blinking, her duty very important.

I love riding my horse Cesa. Her Andalusian stature and Arabian spirit make it seem as though she is a knight's steed straight out of medieval times. Rumer felt that I, too, needed supervision in this, however, thinking it her duty to help control this fiery creature. Leading Cesa along the picture-perfect route from the barn, down the gravel driveway to my riding ring in the front yard, Rumer accompanied us, nudging Cesa's back legs with her tennis ball to move her along. Once in the ring, I rode, first in a circle to warm Cesa up, the "thu thump… thu thump…thu thump" sound I so loved of a perfect canter beating in the dry dust of my ring. Rumer, tennis ball in mouth, ran in circles in the opposite direction on the outside of us, a small cloud of dust puffing under her running paws. Every time we passed, Rumer hopped on stiff front legs, shook her head, and voiced out, "rrrrrr." How annoying it must have been to the horses to have Rumer constantly monitoring their every move, herding them and keeping them in check, if only in her mind.

The Thanksgiving morning of 1997, I woke up early to go out and feed the horses a special holiday breakfast, a nice hot bran and peppermint mash mixed with carrots and apples. I was greeted by Cesa's shrill whinny as I slid open the doors and entered the barn, touching her soft nostrils as she blew out, impatient to eat the steamy, sweet, warm mix I brought. I was blanketing Cesa at that time and, since it was going to be a beautiful day, decided to take her blanket off for a while so she could enjoy the fresh air. I sleepily tried to do this while she was free, without her halter on to hold her. It was very lazy of me and I definitely should have known better. You can never be sure what a horse will do and I learned the hard way that this lazy act on my part was a big mistake.

The blanket that Cesa wore went over her head rather than buckling in the front of her chest. This meant that I had to unbuckle all the leg and belly straps before pulling it over her head to get it off. Cesa, in all her sassiness, decided to trot away from me after I had unbuckled all the clips but hadn't yet pulled the blanket off of her. As she trotted away, I watched in horror as the blanket began to slip sideways, turning to slide to her front. As it made its way around and under her, she tripped on it. As she tripped, it began to tighten around her neck. Needless to say, this caused her to become completely and utterly panic-stricken.

I stood helpless as Cesa took off at full gallop, screaming in panic, trying to get away from this thing that was attacking her. As she ran, she kept tripping on the blanket and falling to her knees, only to keep getting up to run again. I could only watch, hoping she wouldn't go through the fence, knowing if she did there would be nothing stopping her except something tragic.

Thankfully, Cesa made a frantic u-turn to come back toward the barn, still screaming, tripping, falling, and running. She ran into her stall and stood there, a trembling, sweating, panicky mess. In the meantime, Baby, the thoroughbred living with us, heard and saw the "attack" on Cesa and joined in the panic, even though nothing was happening to her. She never hesitated but ran straight through the electric fence and took off through the yard, pulling the whole line of fencing with her. I stood there, mouth open for what seemed a lifetime but was, in reality, a few seconds, trying to get my mind around what had just happened. Finally jumping into action, I realized I could only do one thing at a time. I knew I had to lock Cesa in her stall and get the blanket off of her first. I just prayed she stayed put while I ran to the outside of the barn to close the stall door.

By the time I locked the stall door and reached Cesa, I was trying to control the shaking that began in my body. The blanket was wound so tightly around her neck, I had to cut it off with scissors. Trembling, my knees barely holding me up, I was just able to get the scissors between Cesa's neck and the blanket to begin cutting it off.

Thankfully, Lee both saw and heard this whole sad display from her bedroom at my parents' house and came running to help. Cheryl and my father joined her, both of whom also heard the commotion. Someone was able to catch Baby and return her to her stall. After I made sure Cesa was okay, both horses remained locked in the barn for most of the day while we began fence repairs. It was not the most relaxing Thanksgiving Day.

As soon as everything settled down, I went in the house to get Rumer. She immediately knew something was amiss and charged over to the barn, sniffing the ground and downed fence. Blinking and huffing, she seemed to realize that the horses had somehow escaped. She couldn't believe it! The audacity of the horses getting out the minute she wasn't there to watch them! She couldn't even go to sleep—look at what happened! Spending the rest of the day at her post, Rumer decided she needed to up her hours at monitoring the horses. They obviously could *not* be trusted.

Of equal importance was Rumer's other self-appointed job of nursemaid. She helped Cheryl, her RN mother, with the various maladies that surfaced among my family. Rumer epitomized why pit bulls were nicknamed "nursemaids." She loved, as much as anything, to stay in all day, putting aside her desire to play or to watch the horses, to "nurse" someone's illness. She knew when someone needed her healing presence, from nursing Lee back from a fever, kissing her from head to foot (her form of a sponge bath), to staying by someone's side in bed all day.

"You're the best nurse in the world," I often told Rumer affectionately, of course, winking at Cheryl as I did.

To me, one of the most endearing traits Rumer developed helped to reinforce how kind and considerate she was. Of her own accord, it became a requirement that she greet everyone when she first saw them each day. Each morning, she sought out Cheryl and me, making it a point to come and kiss each of us before going out. She "made the rounds" when at my parents', making a circuit of the house until she found each and every one of my brothers, sisters, mother and father, in order to greet them by licking any piece of exposed skin she could find, laughing as she went. If someone wasn't home at the time and came in the house after she arrived, she got up to greet them in the same way. Every day was a new and wonderful day with the family she loved. She made sure that we all knew how grateful she was that we were all a part of her life.

And, before Rumer left my parents' house, she again "made the rounds" to kiss everyone "goodbye," never missing anyone, including any visitor who was willing to accept this demonstration of her love.

Beautiful summer evenings brought a late midnight blue sky as dusk approached. My family, leaving after a day of fun at the pool, walked away up the gravel drive back home. Everyone said their "goodbyes" to Rumer before leaving, Rumer giving sloppy kisses to all while standing on the deck, late summer golden rays silhouetting her laughing face. After these long "goodbyes," she tried to, as we called it, "sneak off with the crowd," hoping to prolong her wonderful day by sneaking into the middle of my family's pack on their walk back home.

Cheryl and I said, "We see you, Rumer. Don't try to sneak off with the crowd." Still laughing, she kissed everyone "goodbye" all over again, then turned to come back home to await the next wonderful morning when all the fun would begin anew.

With Rumer, it was so easy for us to treat her as a human being because she had so many traits that were "humanlike." Anthropomorphism suggests that we place human characteristics on animals, intentions and emotions that don't belong. But, I know animals have emotions. Human beings are part of the group that we call animals, after all, and they most certainly don't have a monopoly on feelings. Rumer proved to have a sense of appreciation, of being grateful for what she had in life, of understanding hurt feelings and not wanting to "do the wrong thing."

Brown monkey eyes, squinting with intention as she seeks out my eyes. Mornings, after she gets up with me to go potty, I'm drinking my coffee, and feel the heat of her gaze. She inches her way toward the stairway, watching me, knowing Cheryl is up in the bedroom still sleeping and wants to rejoin her for more rest. But, she pauses, looking at me, and then looking longingly and apologetically up the stairs. She keeps doing this, needing my permission in order to leave me.

"It's okay, Rumi. I don't mind—go ahead," I tell her. And, freed from such rudeness as leaving (more mannered than many people) she bounds happily up the stairs and back to bed to cuddle with Cheryl.

We call you "Ru," "Chicopee," "Po-Po," "Sweet Pea," "Rumer-Pot-Pie," "Rumie," "Chicken Little," "Ruzeroozky," "Pork Chop," and "Rumie Frozen Brains." We christen you "Doll Face," "Golden Angel," "Pie Pie," "Pie Pie Pony Dog," "Angel Pie," and "Poke," for how you poke things quickly and pointedly with your nose. I know that you love your nicknames just as much as your true name, for you know that these are only and always meant as the greatest terms of endearment.

CHAPTER 32

Every spring and summer we have a pair of wild mallards that come to stay in Rumer's beloved pond. Rumer spent hours here, swimming to cool off or playing with her tennis ball. Making up her own game when everyone else was busy, she stood in the water and poked the ball with her nose or paw to make it bounce under and float back up at her. When bored with this, she looked out from the water and barked for hours, *demanding* that someone come to throw her ball or stick. She barked so long that my father, who never got mad at her, ended up shouting for her to be quiet.

One afternoon, she persistently kept barking, even through my father's reprimands from the house. He finally had enough and stormed off to the pond to get her, forcing her laughing, slouching self back up the driveway with him to their house. When he later admitted to Diane that he yelled at Rumer that afternoon, she told him that he was mean. Just that little bit of discipline to Rumer was frowned upon!

Every year, "our" ducks have babies in this pond, once having as many as nine little ones. Rumer loved swimming amongst them and they never minded, tranquilly swimming together, dog-with-ball and ducks. It was a wonderful sight.

The only disruption to this tranquility came from an unlikely source, a pair of geese that sometimes flew in to enjoy the pond, too. As time passed, the geese competed for this area, chasing the peaceful ducks, trying to own the pond for themselves. It finally went too far for me when the geese attacked the baby ducks.

It happened one peaceful, quiet summer afternoon as I was cleaning the barn, Rumer lying in front of the horse fence, watching. I heard a horrible racket, a quacking commotion coming from the pond. I ran out to see, shielding my eyes from the bright sun with my arm, trying to make out what was happening. Rumer jumped up, spinning toward the pond to look with me. I saw our mother duck, quacking in fear, trying her hardest to herd her babies to safety away from the attacking geese!

Rumer watched curiously as I yelled, "That's it!" I stomped angrily into the barn to get my rake and hurriedly ran to the duck's rescue, running after the geese, yelling and screaming for them to leave the ducks alone.

The geese ran from me, flapping along the ground around the whole property, but always circling back to the pond, not willing to give up this prime area so easily. I kept chasing them, just as determined to help our ducks as they were to lay claim to the pond. I sank in mud and pond scum halfway up to my knees, splattered from head to foot, all crazy-looking, yelling in anger and chasing a pair of geese all over the property while wielding a rake like a maniac.

Was Rumer the aggressive one? Witnessing, not joining, my angry attack, she probably thought I'd gone crazy.

CHAPTER 33

Lee works for a wonderful husband and wife chiropractor team, Dr. Kay and Dr. Joe. Dr. Kay is not only a great chiropractor, but a photographer to be envied as well. Lee invites Dr. Kay to the house to visit occasionally and to spend time walking the property, enjoying the nature that surrounds us. With its ponds, brooks, fields, and wildlife, the property is a photographer's dream and Dr. Kay takes the most beautiful pictures for us as she and Lee stroll along. Rumer enjoyed Dr. Kay's company and accompanied them on their walks, sticking close by in companionable peace.

One visit, Kay watched Rumer thoughtfully as they walked along, enjoying good conversation with Lee in the fresh, bright, late summer sun. Thinking how beautiful Rumer was, Kay asked Lee, "Do you think I could use Rumer in my shots? I'd love to take some nice pictures of her."

Lee turned to Kay and, with a mischievous glint in her eyes, said, "Why don't you ask Rumer?'

Playing along with what she thought was a joke, Kay turned to Rumer and good-humouredly asked, "Rumer, can I take your picture?"

Kay quickly realized that the joke was on her. Rumer actually *understood* her question, having been asked the same one by Lee so many times. At Kay's question, Rumer looked up at her, ceased her panting for a second and cocked her head to the side, ears perked, then turned and walked to the middle of the field in which they were standing. Once there, she stopped in front of the brook, sat down, and posed with her head facing sideways, just so. The 15-foot tall fronds that grew along the brook bobbed behind her in the breeze, like dancers' heads bopping to the beat of nature's music.

Dr. Kay turned to Lee, mouth open in disbelief. Even seeing it for herself, she could hardly believe this intelligence, this understanding Rumer had. From that point on, Kay always took her pictures with Rumer as the focal point. She placed Rumer on a huge boulder... "Snap". She sat her near the pond, then in the sunflower garden in front of the barn, then next to the cement flower bowl my grandfather had made which was packed full of my mother's purple, fragrant petunias... "Snap...Snap...Snap."

Rumer, almost 6 then, was in her prime and at her most beautiful. She was the epitome of health and happiness, her teeth a brilliant white as she panted with laughter, so outstanding against her muzzle of which was the darkest and fullest black. Her almond-shaped brown eyes squinted with happiness within their mascara-lined lids. Her body was a perfect weight and ratio of muscle, her color an exquisite vanilla, her chest a brilliant white to give her teeth a run for their money.

Dr. Kay is responsible for some of the most beautiful pictures of Rumer we have. They are truly treasured and make up almost all of the photos of her that we've framed. Dr. Kay grew to know and love Rumer, even adorning her chiropractic office with some of these pictures of her. She is a very important person in our lives. She became especially important in Rumer's life later, when Rumer developed debilitating pain. How could we even have guessed back then, when she was a pudgy puppy, a lanky teenager, an exquisitely perfect specimen now in early mid-age, what would become of her?

While Dr. Kay is one very important piece of puzzle in all our lives, another is our vet, Dr. John. I made his acquaintance through one of my farriers. One cold morning, with Rumer watching carefully while I held Cesa for my farrier to fit her with shoes, he told me about Dr. John. Knowing how well we take care of our animals, he said, "I thought you might want to know about a new large animal vet in the area. I've only heard very good things about him from everyone."

That spring, Cheryl and I decided to call Dr. John to set up the horses' annual vet visit. It was the spring of Rumer's 4th year. As soon as he pulled up the gravel drive in his Mitsubishi SUV and got out to warmly greet us, Cheryl and I felt an immediate affinity toward him. Into our lives he came with his floppy brown hair, boyish charm, good looks, and great sense of humor, a Godsend to us all. Down the future road, he became especially important to Rumer.

Seeing Rumer and the two horses in our yard, he asked what other animals we had. We told him about our three cats after which he said, "I'm also a small animal vet, so, if you'd like, I can take care of all your animals when I come out for the horses."

Cheryl and I looked at each other. Could this be true?! "Yes!" we said in unison. "We'd LOVE that!"

Imagine…not having to take our animals to the vet anymore, that horrible, yowling, howling, nerve-wracking drive. He would be coming to us! Another bonus was that Dr. John was on call for emergencies—how utterly invaluable. An almost unheard of extra bonus was that he practiced alternative and holistic remedies! We couldn't believe our luck.

On this first visit, after inspecting and giving the required shots to the horses and before he left, Dr. John sat in his SUV, facing out as he wrote up our bill. Pointing at Rumer he said, "You know, it's unconstitutional for breed-specific bans. If you ever run into a problem, remember that."

For just this small bit of support, I was so very grateful, and it only got better from there. He has allowed me such peace of mind over and over again through the years because of his philosophy and willingness to help in any way necessary for an animal's benefit. From that very first meeting, my whole family began a great relationship with Dr. John. Rumer, however, never fully trusted him and just couldn't seem to stop barking at him. Even when put in the house, her incessant "whoof…whoof…whoof" could be heard until he pulled back out of our driveway and sped off to his next appointment.

Each spring, he came to give all the animals their shots and checkups. As he started with the horses, Rumer watched him closely, holding her tennis ball, shaking her head, and making her "rrrrrrrr" noise if the horses misbehaved at all. Then, Dr. John moved on to all the cats: Taja, Lily, and Monnie. Finally, it was Rumer's turn. Oh, she was so upset with Cheryl and me when we corralled her and made her sit on the patch of grass in front of the barn where Douglas, the fir tree, was planted. Dr. John gently checked her over, poking and prodding, checking her ears, eyes, and teeth. Rumer barely sat to tolerate this violation from him and her disapproval of us for allowing it was abundantly clear. She accepted it obediently only because we asked it of her.

As part of the checkup, Dr. John needed to draw Rumer's blood for her heartworm test. I held Rumer around her chest while Dr. John gently took her front paw and drew blood through the nice large vein in Rumer's upper arm. Rumer turned her head to the side so she didn't have to witness this new, additional violation. When Dr. John finished collecting the blood, he placed a bandage on Rumer's upper forearm at the needle site, Rumer barely able to sit still. As soon as she was released, she jumped up, hopped away, and started her continuous barking as she looked back over her shoulder at him. She nailed him with her famous sideways look, only she put as much disdain in this look as she could muster.

Without realizing it at first, the bandaging of Rumer's arm on these occasions became very important in proving how sensitive she really was. This bandage consisted of a cotton ball at the needle site held in place around her upper forearm by medical tape. Each year, we all made a big "to do" about her "boo boo." We looked at the bandage and cooed sympathetically. We held up her paw, kissed it, and murmured consoling sounds. We kept this bandage on Rumer for days to make up for what had been done. By the time we took it off, the bandage was dirty and frayed, hanging on by a thread.

After a few years of this, however, we realized a peculiar thing. Rumer acted strangely every time we had to bandage her for some reason. It was as if making a big deal about it made her actually become physically ill. She moped around, acted lethargic, didn't eat, and just *became* sick. It was so extreme that we had to stop drawing any attention to bandages and, as soon as we possibly could, remove any bandages that we absolutely *had* to put on her. Rumer was just too sensitive, more sensitive than many people I've known…my sweet, gentle soul.

Eventually, Dr. John opened a small animal clinic. When this happened, we had to bring the cats and Rumer to him. But in the meantime, it worked so well.

CHAPTER 34

Late summer into the fall of 1998, Taja, my wolf kitty, became very sick. She had been losing weight steadily for some time, which she couldn't afford, and was put on medication for an infection. By the weekend before Thanksgiving, she was skin and bones and walked the property in a daze. That Sunday, I didn't want to let her out of the house in the state she was in, so afraid that I would never see her again. I eventually gave in to her insistence though, as she cried and begged to go. I knew that being outside was what made her happiest in life. Being among nature hunting and watching, sitting or stalking, were her favorite activities and I just couldn't take that away from her.

By late afternoon, there was no sign of her and I became very worried. I looked for her and called to her, walking the yard, searching all her favorite spots in hopes of finding her. My search proved fruitless, however, and after a while I gave up and made my way to the barn. I climbed the stairway to the loft, avoiding my family and Cheryl in my sadness. I sat for a long time among the bales of hay, breathing in great breaths of sweet smells, rays of sunlight streaking through the barn board cracks to warm my skin, my face raised to feel their reach. I drew comfort from this, from where Taja so loved to sleep. After sitting there for a long time, I sighed and rose, finally going back home to wait, resigned to the fact that I might never see her again.

Periodically, I searched the yard from the house windows, hoping to see Taja's familiar sight. And, as early evening approached, to my joy, yet heartache, I did see her, approaching the house from the front woods, coming up the driveway in a daze, still. I ran outside as quickly as I could to meet her and pick her up to carry her inside. Although I was as gentle as could be, she cried in pain as I did so.

Once we had her inside, Cheryl and I then began the difficult task of trying to get her to eat something, anything. We went through all of her most favorite dishes in order to entice her: 6 second cream (half and half warmed up just right at 6 seconds in the microwave), half raw beef chunks, wet cat food… but, nothing worked. My heart broke when she wouldn't eat at all.

She finally settled into a fitful sleep, curling into a little ball in her favorite spot for the evening, our loft room. I approached her later that night and kneeled in front of her, tears in my eyes, as I tried to get her to eat again. I was overjoyed when she finally took about a quarter-size amount of soft food from my fingers. But, Cheryl and I knew intuitively that she was suffering greatly. So, the next morning, Monday, Cheryl called Dr. John to ask him if he could come to our house that day to end Taja's pain. He agreed to come that night after his calls.

I couldn't even think about going to work that day and called out sick to be with my Taja. Rumer knew something was wrong and stayed home with us, not willing to miss something so important and a chance to comfort when it was so needed by both Taja and me. Taja kept asking to go outside throughout the morning, but I made her stay in this time, though it was so hard. She eventually gave up and went back to the loft to curl up and go to sleep.

Rumer and I went outside together later that afternoon, quietly sneaking outside as Taja slept so as not to disturb her. After playing "stick" with me and then watching me for a while, knowing my heart wasn't in the mood to play, Rumer asked me if she could go to Grammie's. I took her sweet head in my hands and said, "Go ahead, Ru. Go have fun at Grammie's." She looked in my eyes, squinting in that thoughtful way that defined her, and turned to walk across the field while I began to dig Taja's grave.

Taja's favorite spot was the hillside in front of our barn which sloped beautifully down to the front brook. There in the high grasses and copse of trees, Taja sat for hours, her tortoiseshell coloring blending into the surroundings, a cat statue patiently hunting the moles, chipmunks, and squirrels that made the mistake of passing her way. I chose the exact spot where she liked to sit, and began to dig. After I thought the grave was deep enough, I retrieved a bucket from the barn and collected pinecones and pine needles and clean, fresh leaves with which to make a nice soft bed for her. I placed the bucket there, beside the grave, in waiting. Wiping the dirt off my hands onto my warm-ups and surveying what I had done, I turned, walked back to the house, and went in to spend some time with Taja. Oh, the waiting was so very hard.

At the first hint of dusk, I heard Rob approaching on his walk down to the barn with Rumer. He stopped to say "hi" to the horses, and then began to play roof ball with Rumer. Taja was finally resting comfortably, so I got up from the living room couch to look out the side window to watch them. I had forgotten that Rumer held a great hatred for buckets. By the time I looked out, Rumer had spotted the hateful bucket, boldly sitting in plain view, full of pinecones and pine needles. I watched, hand over my open mouth, as she grabbed it and began running all over the yard, flipping and shaking it in play as she went. All my beautiful, soft pinecones, pine needles, and leaves were strewn from one end of the yard to the other. Rob, not knowing that they had been collected for a specific reason, just watched and laughed.

I ran outside to stop her but, by that time, not even a speck of what I had lovingly collected was left in the bucket. As Rumer obligingly let me take the bucket back after having her fill of fun, I noticed that the bucket itself was ripped and littered with tooth punctures. I couldn't help it. I kneeled down in front of Rumer, hugged her panting body, and laughed with her while she blessed me with kisses, such loving benedictions reaching to my very soul. Even without realizing it (or, maybe she had), at one of the worst times in my life, Rumer still made me laugh. I went out to recollect everything and, this time, I put the bucket out of Rumer's sight and reach.

After Taja died, I had panic attacks at night. Taja, my cute, funny, so-smart little bug, had been with me for 12 ½ of the hardest years of my life, from my early 20's to my early 30's. She moved with me from apartment to apartment, to Florida for 3 months, and finally to our wonderful property. It was unfathomable that she was gone. I lay awake at night, unable to fall asleep. I got a tingly, dizzy feeling, and almost fainted from lack of air. I lurched up into a sitting position in bed, gasping, finally getting up, pacing the house to try to stop the panic. When I did fall asleep, I had terrible dreams about Taja. I dreamed that she hadn't really been dead when we buried her that night, Cheryl and I hugging and kissing her body, cradling her lovingly before placing her in her grave on that clear, crisp evening with starlight our only illumination, our tears flowing over her beautiful, lovingly-tended fur.

I dreamed that she was trying to dig her way out of the hole in which we had buried her, or that she was back, dirty from her grave, but alive. I dreamed of crying, either grief-filled for her loss or with happiness at seeing her again. I knew that I held a great deal of guilt over the decision to put her to sleep and was not bearing this responsibility well. This was especially difficult for me since she had not wanted to go and painfully fought, to the very end, the relaxant that was given to her. I was now haunted, and, nighttime was the worst.

What helped me through this horrible time was Rumer. For those few awful months after Taja's death, I placed my hand on Rumer's sleeping body every night, drawing from her the comfort that I needed, her beautiful, rhythmic breathing lulling me to sleep. Her soft snoring, along with her strong, solid body, calmed my panic and steadied my emotions.

From that point forward, I developed a deeply vital habit of touching any part of her body that I could reach, a habit that became as essential to me as breathing. So, on Rumer is where my hand stayed every night until her last year when her body, swollen and hot from cancer and prednisone, became so uncomfortable that she couldn't stand the pressure. She couldn't tolerate any touch, even one that was light as a feather, so I had to draw on my own strength for her. It was hard not to touch her by then. She had given me an irreplaceable sense of peace for so long. But, by then, she had also changed me as a person, lending me a strength of spirit and character that I never would have gained without her. By that point, I could do this for her, be strong for her, be a source of comfort for *her*. Through our years together, I had the best teacher, after all.

After Taja's death, life slowly returned to normal with Rumer's help and strong spiritual presence. The next few, beautiful years seemed to fly by. The seasons rapidly passed with a few wonderful constants marking time, resulting in a beautiful routine. The magnificent sight and sound of honking geese leaving in fall and returning in spring every year, our property part of their route, were as reliable as the sun rising every morning. I never tired of standing beneath a flock as they flew over, listening to the sound, a whispering, almost whistling "phum...

phum…phum" of their powerful wings as they passed. The return of "my" barn swallows every spring filled me with happiness. Back they would come every late April or early May, swooping in with such joy and exuberance, ready to build their nest and honor us by having their babies in our welcoming barn. The most important constant, though, the rock of strength in all our lives was Rumer. It seemed that we had Rumer whole and healthy for a much shorter amount of time than it was. Happiness has a way of doing that, of making time seem to go by so much faster than sorrow.

After these beautiful years, Cheryl and I found ourselves entering a new stage with Rumer, a stage that we first entered oblivious to the test it would prove to be for us as loving and patient parents. For, Rumer began to develop serious health issues as she approached later middle age. By seven years old, she developed debilitating arthritis and, soon after, benign fatty tumors that would eventually betray their "benignness." Previously a specimen of complete beauty and grace, her body began a downhill slide, slowly but surely inhibiting her favorite activities and basic quality of life.

How would we as parents try to help her? How much did we love her? Enough to spend countless amounts of money, enough to spend countless sleepless nights, enough to give her all the love and patience and strength that she had given us unconditionally for so many years, enough to helplessly and painfully watch her condition degenerate? Enough to bear witness to her stoic attitude through it all and how she asked for nothing although she needed so much?

Thus began the cruelness for which life can be known. Only, it was cruelness to one of the most innocent, considerate, loving souls I ever knew.

My beautiful girl, sitting in the warm, healing sun, looking out over the yard as I stare at you in adoration. I can see your whiskers, most black, some now turned white, outlined in the bright rays, gleaming porcupine quills. You are sweet and altruistic beyond measure and you laugh and laugh as I kiss your soft muzzle, feeling the sharp pricks of those whiskers. You think you are so funny, your life always lived with such a keen sense of humor. You make me laugh even when I'm not ready to. You are my gift from life.

CHAPTER 35

As Rumer passed her seventh birthday, her once strong, athletic body, a body that could leap straight up in the air to kiss your face without laying a paw on you, revealed signs of debilitating arthritis. It was so slight at first, this arthritis—a limp here, soreness for a few days there, an occasional struggle to get on the couch. We explained it away for a while as discomfort brought on by her very active lifestyle.

It was Rumer's wrists, her beautiful vanilla wrists that finally gave it away and made us see the issue for what it was. Her wrists bothered her, especially at night, and she licked them for hours, trying to sooth them. Then, it happened during the day, too, the licking for hours, just the same spots over and over, in soothing repetition. Eventually, her wrists revealed the pain within, arthritis raising its ugly head in the form of knotty, deformed, swollen bones.

As her arthritis worsened, Rumer was extremely sore for days, sometimes barely able to walk if she exerted herself physically. We often resorted to putting her in the house when she wouldn't stop playing when we asked.

Lee kept Dr. Kay informed of Rumer's pain level. When it started getting worse, Dr. Kay asked, "Why don't you have Jolene and Cheryl bring Rumer in to be x-rayed? We'll at least be able to tell if something else is happening internally."

Cheryl and I jumped at this wonderful offer. We made an appointment to bring Rumer for x-rays on one of our vacation days that summer of 2000. Rumer proved to be a trooper through the whole process. The car ride wasn't nearly as bad as we thought (Taja's horrible yowling not adding to the mix and egging on Rumer's own terror as when we traveled to the vet) and when it came to the x-ray process itself, Rumer stood calmly where we placed her. She allowed us to manipulate her body in different positions in order to get the x-rays of her whole hip and spine area. I stayed with her, holding her closely against my chest, wearing the protective x-ray vest Dr. Kay buckled on me.

After all the x-rays were taken, Cheryl, Lee, and I nervously awaited the results. Dr. Kay meticulously combed through them then approached where we waited and said, "Well, Rumer seems to have nothing else wrong with her. There's nothing out of place. She's just dealing with arthritis right now."

It was just your basic, degenerative arthritis.

Once we learned this, we did everything we could to help Rumer with her pain level. Cheryl and I researched arthritis in dogs and spoke to other people who had animals with arthritis. All of our research pointed us in the direction of a holistic remedy called glucosamine. Testimonials revealed how glucosamine could do wonders for dogs as well as people with arthritis problems, a "miracle" treatment some called it. We gave it to Rumer in every meal right away with high hopes that this would help her. To our joy, the glucosamine did work. Rumer was, once again, able to run upstairs, jump on the couch without help, or chase the horses with little pain and soreness after. Her wrists weren't so swollen and knotty.

We also made sure that she received chiropractic care from Dr. Kay and another family friend, Dr. Mina. Even further, Cheryl and I contacted our massage therapist, Monique, to ask if she could help. "Well, now I can tell people I've had the experience of massaging a pit bull!" Monique joked the day she came to our house, as if an indication of her bravery.

Rumer loved her massage and fell in love with Monique because of it. She lay where we put her on the nice thick loft carpeting, allowing us to move her side-to-side, limbs pulled and tugged, body probed and kneaded. She just lay limp and appreciative, sighing with bliss. Monique was kind enough to show Cheryl and me how to perform these massages with Rumer ourselves, so that we could continue this therapy for her.

In these ways, we were able to hold Rumer's arthritis at bay for a while. In order to continue in our endeavor to help, Cheryl and I made the decision in 2002 to purchase an in-ground pool to take the place of our on-side pool. Our hope was that, with an in-ground pool and its stairway into the water, Rumer could swim herself. Swimming provided a wonderful activity while keeping the stress off her arthritic joints.

Only too quickly, glucosamine began to lose its effectiveness for Rumer. We tried everything else we could think of to help her live life as normally as possible. We bought a dog ramp so she could still get on the bed on her own. We helped her on and off everything like the couch and golf cart. Regardless of our efforts, her pain still progressed to the point where she couldn't make it up the stairs to bed anymore unless I carried her. We finally called Dr. John.

It was a dreadful call, it was a call that admitted defeat to Rumer's growing health problem. Sitting at the dining room table, ready to write everything down with pad and paper, I dialed Dr. John's number. When he came to the phone with his usual warm welcome, I told him about Rumer's pain. I explained everything we had tried, everything we were doing to help her have a better quality of life, but she now needed more than what we could do. Dr. John, after voicing how impressed he was with our efforts, enlightened us to the different pain medication options available. He patiently explained each treatment and the health risks each could pose.

Cheryl and I found ourselves on the cusp of a downward spiral of Rumer's accumulating health problems. We found ourselves approaching that cliff, our stomachs flipping as we gazed warily and fearfully over and down an unavoidable road, a road that continued to bring us to the same predicament over and over: having to weigh the quality of life for Rumer with giving her various medications for her health issues.

After Dr. John explained everything, he sensed our hesitation and the great worry we held. He said, "Why don't you both think it over. Call me back when you're ready, okay?"

That evening, Cheryl and I spent much time thinking and talking about our choices. In the end, sitting there in bed discussing Rumer's future, it was Rumer herself who made our decision. Close to an hour after we began talking about our opinions, we just stopped and looked at her. What we saw and heard made our decision without another hesitant thought, without any regret: Rumer, licking and licking her sore, swollen, inflamed wrists, trying in vain to find relief from the pain.

The next morning, we called Dr. John with our decision to start Rumer on Rimadyl. We accepted the fact that it might harm Rumer's liver in the long run. Her quality of life was what we agreed upon as the most important issue in making decisions for her. Cheryl and I, along with Dr. John, vowed never to let Rumer have pain or suffer unnecessarily. This was always our top priority to the very end.

Rumer's debilitating arthritis was difficult for all of us, including my family. It altered her life in many ways and was a visible reminder of her pain to those who loved her so much. But, we took it in stride and adjusted everything around her to help. What proved to be even worse, however, were the lumps that appeared on her body. Like good mothers, Cheryl and I knew every inch of Rumer, any new cut or scrape, anything out of the ordinary. These lumps started out very small, just little lumps on her sides, on her belly, in between her thighs, and in her groin area. We kept track of them and the next time Dr. John came to look at the horses we had him check these lumps on Rumer.

The day he came, Rumer unhappily but obediently stood on the front porch while Dr. John felt each lump. He took much time and great care to check them thoroughly. On his knees, feeling every one, he said to Cheryl and me, standing there nervously watching, "They're just fatty tumors. They're benign at this point, so just keep an eye on them."

We did, Cheryl routinely checking these "fatty" tumors, making sure that they stayed the same size and shape. They didn't grow, they didn't seem to bother her, and although we noticed a few more develop, they didn't seem to interfere with her life by any means—not like the arthritis.

So, Rumer continued on with her beautiful life and we, seeming to have her arthritis and tumors under control, went on as well. We turned not quite a blind eye, but at least a nearsighted eye, to Rumer's health problems. Although these health problems seemed to be mounting, we only focused on the good we still had, the road we presently traversed. And, that good was the fact that Rumer brought so much to our family, completed our whole, brought us more joy and love than anything else in our lives.

I sometimes look back and regret so much. Although Rumer taught me to appreciate everything in the future, I hadn't yet quite learned this important lesson. I would do so, Rumer would show me, but I'm tortured by my ignorance of Rumer's mortality at that time. Why hadn't I appreciated more her once-strong body, pre-tumors, pre-sores, pre-drugbloat, so athletic and exquisite? When I look back through pictures of her from her baby years through her teen and early mid-years, I see her beautiful, healthy body. I see the spark, the *life* that emanated from her.

Why didn't I appreciate so much more our time together, time that I didn't need to give her so many pills, time without her weeping sores, without the tumors that grew so large that they pushed her limbs out at unnatural angles, time without the skin tags and moles growing on her, without her joints deformed with pain? How does one go from such perfection to such deterioration in such a short amount of time? Every day, I should have appreciated her beauty, her strength, her carefree days. We get so carried away with the stresses of everyday life that we don't appreciate the present, the life we have *now*, the life that truly matters.

I so hope that Rumer knew how very much I loved her.

LATER

Rumer, my love, my beautiful, vanilla-carmel girl, sunning yourself in front of the barn amongst the flowers or, even better, amongst the horse poop. You smell like fresh-cut grass, baked pork, and a hint of unmentionables. Ever watchful of us all, you are so happy doing what you do. When I sit beside you now and hug your strong body, I can feel the slight lumps and bumps of your tumors as my hands travel lovingly over your neck, shoulders, and back. I cannot even think about what this means yet. Your value in my life is greater than any amount of treasure I can fathom…more than a cavernous room full of the finest-spun gold.

CHAPTER 36

When are the best years of our lives? How do we know... how do we recognize them? Have we already lived them, are we presently in them, are they yet to come?

I still remember the day that I had to start walking with Rumer to my parents' house, accompanying her on her pilgrimage. It was that dreadful fall, the fall she was diagnosed with cancer, the fatty tumors no longer benign. In the fall of 2003, when she was given until spring, at most, to live.

By that time, we talked to Rumer and she actually understood. We had discussions with her and she lay there listening, looking back with her sideways look, laughing appropriately at something funny, or listening in shared sympathy at something sad. We just thought something and she acknowledged it...and vice versa. We all knew her so well that we knew what she wanted and when she was trying to tell us something. We only had to watch, to listen.

It was a morning that revealed the beginning of fall, the kind of glorious, beautiful morning that makes one excited to be alive. The brilliant, rising sun was just beginning to touch the various shades of golds and reds of the trees that lined the front of the barn, wisps of steam rising from the trunks as the rays found the dampness there to warm. The air was fresh, cool, as I breathed in great breaths. Rumer came out to the barn with me that morning, as usual, the sweet smells of hay and horse greeting us as I rolled open the barn doors to hungry neighing. She watched me clean the stalls for a while, biding her time before meandering off to Grammie's, probably dreaming of all the new scents she'd have to investigate that had gathered overnight in the field across the way. Maybe she would be so lucky as to find some nice goose poop to roll in or eat.

But, that particular morning proved different. I felt it before I saw it. I stopped what I was doing and turned to lock gazes with the most beautiful brown eyes I had ever seen. With an intense look from her, I realized that she needed something, maybe the usual reassurance about leaving me. I said to her, "Go ahead, Rumie Pie. It's okay—I love you. Have a good day at Grammie's and I'll see you tonight" as I walked a few steps with her.

When I turned back to continue my chores, she stopped as well, turning ponderously to look back at me. I stopped again and looked at her. As I looked into her too-intelligent eyes and she into mine, I noticed that she *really* looked at me, squinting oh-so-slightly in concentration, ears perked in their "flying nun" position.

"What is it, Rumie?" I asked her, trying to figure out what was wrong.

I stared at her, she stared back in her squinting way, head cocked slightly to the side. Then, it came to me. She wanted me to walk with her all the way to Grammie's and she was asking in the only way she knew how. She knew herself so well by this time, knew that the deterioration of her body condition was so extreme, that she could no longer trust herself to make it to Grammie's alone. She needed me there with her in case she couldn't make it, and though I can't imagine what it took for this strong-willed girl, she asked me for help.

"Okay, let's go—I'll take you," I said to her as lightly and as nonchalantly as I could although I felt my heart break.

And, so I did, walking oh-so-slowly to match her limping gait, stray leaves gently fluttering down around us as gently as a soft rain. On our way, she looked at me occasionally in that beloved sideways glance of hers, eyes half closed, and I looked back at her to catch her eye, trying not to let her see the tears threatening. On most of these walks, I found myself singing to her from the deepest part of my heart:

You are my sunshine my only sunshine
You make me happy when skies are gray
You'll always know, Dear, how much I love thee,
Please don't take my sunshine away.

She shuffled along to my song, her left back toes occasionally dragging in the gravel due to the huge tumor in her left inner thigh, so big that her back leg was out at an angle that made her slip or become unbalanced.

I always made it seem as though it was something I wanted to do and not something that she needed me to do, strolling to Grammie's at a snail's pace every morning when I had so much other work. Oh, how much it took for her to start giving in to this evil affliction, how much it took from her to know innately that her once-remarkable strength was no longer what it used to be, her health so deteriorated that she needed her mother near in case she fell.

Through it all, on those slow walks, Rumer's brown almond eyes catching mine every now and then, yawning, impatient to be there already where she would just go to sleep again with Diane or my father, I remember coming to a life-changing realization. It was an epiphany, really, a wave bowling me over, roaring so loudly that it blocked out all other thought, so totally encompassing that I stumbled a little. I was in the midst of living the best years of my life, right now. My life was presently full of more love than it would ever be again.

I felt my eyes fill with tears as I thought about it. All that I love, all that I cherish in my life are with me, right now: Cheryl, my parents, my siblings, my Rumer Pie, my animals. Oh, what those walks gave me, afforded me. Something that I started doing because I had to, for Rumer, became something that I *did* want to do. These morning walks allowed me to find the joy in slowing down, spending and savoring those precious times with her, the one I loved so much. It wasn't Pepper and Kitty anymore sitting together with me on an old dirt mound in a farmer's field watching the sunrise, but me and my Rumer, limping our way up the gravel road to Grammie's.

On those walks I felt the stresses of life draining away, transporting me to the joys of childhood again. I felt the morning sunlight on my face, acknowledged the blue of the sky, a shade that just can't be duplicated, smelled the odors of our earth. I was reminded of all that truly matters in life, felt what was true and loving and good before having to go to work. I re-learned how important it is to slow down and experience these precious moments, moments that will never be able to be relived, that will be gone forever once we let them go. Suddenly, as one who was never known for patience in the past and having been prone to annoyance over trivial things, I found myself blessed with infinite peace.

Every morning, I received these new lessons, this gift from Rumer, lessons on what really matters in life, Rumer still giving even in her need. Yes, she was sick. Yes, she was hurting, maybe even tiring of this hard and painful life, but she was *here*, still a part of my life, sharing everything from my happiness to my sadness. I could still hug her warm body and hold her chiseled head in my hands to stare into her adoring eyes for comfort and love. Those few moments every morning before work, my time with Rumer, each of us pretending all was well with the world, being strong for each other, were beyond any value I can even imagine. I was living the best moments of my life and I had finally learned, Rumer my Life-Teacher had finally reached me, to savor and treasure them. I learned to live in the most joyous moment, at least for that small amount of time.

I expressed to Rumer this profound truth as she limped along painfully beside me, "These are the best years of my life, Dollface, right now, right here with you and all that I love." And, I truly believed this with my whole, heavy heart.

So, I took it, all I could, sucked as much in as Rumer unconditionally gave me. And, I wanted to give back to her even a small part of what she was giving to me. I would go on forever this way, not caring that she needed so very much. She gave back so much more. I willed time to slow down, to stop. Of course, it couldn't. So, I cherished all that I had, no matter the conditions, because I now knew that it wasn't to be forever.

These later memories of Rumer are so much clearer. The trauma, the tragedy, as well as the recentness, make them so. But I wouldn't take a million dollars for the loss of a single one of these memories of her, no matter how sad. Which memory would I choose to give up, which the least valuable, which any less important than another? They all made up my life with her, the sad as well as the happy, making life with her what it was. Taking any one away would make my life less complete, a cavernous hole where that memory softly lies. I could take these painful memories because they were still of *her*. My love for her was so complete that I would bear whatever pain I had to for her, the pain itself an affirmation of my great love for her. But thankfully, I had another few years with Rumer before the pain and heartache began to infringe upon the joy and happiness.

CHAPTER 37

With the coming of 2002, Cheryl and I were greeted with a wonderful surprise in our lives. We began a new relationship with Cheryl's sister Wendy, our brother-in-law Lorenzo, and their child, our niece, Selena. We all developed a very deep and loving relationship.

It was the first time we met Selena, who was then 8 years old. Selena is one of the nicest, smartest, and most well-grounded kids I've ever known. Cheryl and I were very lucky that Selena loved us and enjoyed visiting and staying with us on weekends that fit into her schedule. She fell in love with our loft room and claimed it for her own.

Rumer immediately developed a loving relationship with Wendy, Lorenzo, and Selena, as well, and loved them as members of her family. Unfortunately, it was so late in Rumer's life that they had not known her as we had. They never knew her in the full grandeur and splendor of her prime. They could only witness her younger beauty in the pictures we showed them and try to comprehend how the beautiful, young body depicted in those pictures could now look like it did. I am just grateful that they got to know *her*, her spirit, her inner beauty and strength, no matter what the exterior revealed.

As we all continued our lives together, the status quo unchanging, Cheryl's family now made a wonderful addition to the mix. We loved them and loved what they brought to our whole—it was so much. The New England seasons brought us beautiful diversity as each one passed, and we all continued happily on, Rumer included. All of our lives were very blessed.

CHAPTER 38

Interrupting this happy existence, the summer of 2003 brought us an unexpected loss. Our little gray kitty, Monnie, tempted by the supreme hunting and the call of a gorgeous summer evening, asked to go out one night...and never returned.

I was scheduled to see Dr. Joe, my chiropractor for whom Lee worked, the next morning. I immediately knew that something was wrong when I looked at Lee's face. She followed me into the adjustment room before Dr. Joe came in and I turned to her, waiting to hear what was wrong. I was shocked when she said, "I'm so worried about Monnie, Jo. She went out last night and hasn't come home."

Although this worried me, too, I said, "Don't worry, Lee. Monnie does this sometimes. I'm sure she'll be back."

But Lee was adamant, knowing. Monnie was really Lee's cat and most attached to her. With tears in her eyes and shaking her head "no" she said, "She doesn't do this. She always comes back in the mornings before I leave for work."

Sadly, Lee turned out to be right. Monnie never came back. It was August when she disappeared. We spent days making up flyers with her picture and a reward, distributing them to every mailbox within a few miles. We walked the property and woods daily, calling to her, checking under rocks, behind trees, in little coves under old entangled tree roots.

Cheryl and I alternated going to the local SPCA on our lunches, going every day for the next 3-4 weeks to see if Monnie turned up. She never did. Our little vagabond was gone. That little terror that had tortured poor Rumer, Taja, and Lily but at the same time had been so very loving, wasn't among us any more. It was very sad not to know what had become of her. Not ever having found her left us always wondering and in limbo, worried about what really happened. We could only assume what had happened to her, the greatest assumptions, that she fell victim to the numerous coy dogs that populated our woods, or was just sick and left to die. But, we were never *sure*.

My family was heartbroken over the loss of Monnie. Not having a cat in the house was very difficult for them. Of course, Monnie acted more like their dog. She accompanied everyone on walks, rode the golf cart, waited up for those who came home late, slept with them, and just kept them company no matter what they were doing. She even pottied outside so that my family never had need of owning a litter box. They all started talking about how "the house wasn't the same" and "maybe we should get another cat."

So torn, their expectations for a new cat were set very high, however. As they talked about it, they ticked off on their fingers their requirements: it had to be two cats, but they'd have to be sisters; they couldn't be kittens, but they couldn't be full-grown; one must be gray with longish fur and the other had to look like Monnie. As such demands increased, they were fast becoming an impossibility to meet. On the one hand, they all wanted new cats so much, but on the other, they so desperately did not ever want to replace Monnie. I'm sure the hope in the back of their minds was that Monnie might even return.

As this play went back and forth, I was struck by the memory of two young cats that I had seen on one of my trips to the SPCA to look for Monnie. I especially remembered them because one looked so much like Monnie, so much so that I had to look through the cage very closely at her to rule it out, the other a beautiful all-gray. They were 8-month-old sisters and met every one of my family's demands.

When I told my family about them one Sunday at dinnertime, my mother, the animal-lover her whole life and still heartbroken over the fact that her family had to kill and eat her pet goat during the Depression, immediately wanted to go adopt them. I made plans with my mother to meet her at the SPCA one day on my lunch to help. She loved these two kitties at first sight. She signed all the paperwork and took home two beautiful sisters: Honey and Sweetie.

I grudgingly admit I was a little worried about how Rumer would react to two new animals. I was afraid that she might not want to share her home. I thought that she might take this out aggressively with the cats, you know, the "don't ever leave your pit bull alone with your cat" horrible philosophy that people hear and repeat all the time. I fell victim to it myself. I spent more time worrying about Rumer's reaction to Honey and Sweetie than anything else. All my worries tunneled into this one issue unnecessarily, for I soon realized that I needn't have worried at all.

These two kitties dropped in on Rumer completely and unexpectedly, blindsiding her at her worst and sickest time. Yet, from the very beginning, it's as if Rumer knew they were meant to be among us. Far from acting aggressively, she accepted it as if it had always been that way and loved the company of the two sisters right from the start. She didn't even mind it when Honey and Sweetie would literally run over her sleeping body as they chased each other in play. And, ironically, it was reverse aggression that actually transpired.

Although Honey is a sweet soul and loved Rumer immediately, Sweetie, the "baby" of the two sisters, proved to be horribly aggressive toward Rumer. Even though Rumer had "seniority" in the house, Sweetie held a grudge against her from the very first. Many times and without instigation, she, as Rumer lay sleeping on the couch, angrily approached the snoring Rumer. She stalked up to her, ears flattened sideways, fur puffed out, tail twitching back and forth, and stopped in front of her. She stared at Rumer angrily for a few minutes, willing her to wake up and start a fight. When this didn't happen, she swatted Rumer's sleeping head, quick and hard swats with nails at full extension, in complete anger. Rumer woke with a start at the slaps, but never retaliated. Most of the time, she laughed in good humor at this disrespectful action. The rest of us were much more upset with Sweetie than she.

Once in a while, my sisters caught Sweetie standing in front of Rumer, one paw raised threateningly, ears flat back to her head, ready to strike. "Sweetie!" they yelled, "Stop that!" And, Sweetie ran, back humped, ears flat, tail wagging murderously, so angry that she was interrupted.

You would think that by now, having lived with a "pit bull" for 12 years and having known many others, I would have given Rumer the credit she deserved for being the beautiful soul she was. All of the bad reputation, all of the negative press, affected even me, one who lived with this angel. So, I can't imagine what it does to people who don't know them. This was a huge change for Rumer, especially at this point in her life. She, as usual, was unbelievable in her acceptance and generosity. I was very much shamed by my own bias.

Embarrassed and wanting to make this up to her, I began to tell her all the time how much I loved her, how so very happy she made me, and how so very proud of her I was. Even though she was hurting, she still tried to make us all laugh with her eternally youthful antics. One thing she especially still loved was to try to get up on my mother's dining room bench so she could sit at the table as we ate dinner and dessert, knowing we'd laugh. Left over from her puppy days when Grammie would carry her around in the crook of her arm and sit at the table while holding her, Rumer still enjoyed trying to get to this vantage point.

My family was in the midst of its usual gathering one Sunday at dinnertime, lasagna, mashed potatoes, ham, and broccoli with cheese sauce adorning the table, loud talk and laughter abundant. At first I didn't notice Rumer, up to her usual trick of trying to scratch and scrape her way onto the slippery dining room bench in between Cheryl and me. As she became more desperate, I finally noticed what she was attempting and decided to help her.

"I'll help you, Rumie," I said as I put my left arm around her rear end and tried to lift her. She scrambled a bit, gaining new purchase with the sudden help, her front claws digging into the slippery bench, so trusting of my help. Finding her much too heavy and big for me to lift by this time, I felt my strength waning, waning…Gone! We all watched in horror, Lee covering her mouth with one hand, everyone else gasping, as Rumer fell straight over backwards in slow motion, flipping back over my useless arm.

Crash… she landed stiffly on her back, legs straight up, amidst the magazine rack behind us, books, magazines, and newspapers flying everywhere in a cascade of noise and chaos. Luckily, she just missed hitting and possibly going through a low window in the wall behind us.

The commotion was followed by a few seconds of quiet, nobody moving, everyone gathering courage to go check on her amongst all the magazines as papers fluttered noiselessly around Rumer's still form. Then, motion once again as everyone ran all at once to Rumer's downed body. She struggled to rise and, as she did so, laughed and laughed, panting in her usual good-natured humor. When we saw this and were sure that she had not been hurt, Lee's hands lovingly traversing every inch of Rumer's body to make sure, my family laughed, too. I looked around nervously at everyone, my eyes eventually finding my beloved, and finally joined in with some nervous laughter of my own.

There I was, still and always, feeling the negligent mother.

CHAPTER 39

As the fall of 2003 approached, Rumer's increasingly painful condition brought us that age-old question: "How can someone so good, someone that gave so much their whole life, suffer so?"

And, suffer Rumer did. Her fatty tumors grew. Her inner left thigh already hosted a massive tumor that continued to get bigger and bigger, separating her back legs in an unnatural way. She had an enormous tumor on her neck and numerous other bumps riddled her body.

At first, I wondered at Rumer's happiness through all of her pain and suffering. I couldn't seem to understand it, how happy she could be all the time. Facing all her pain, the knowledge of her impending death, she was *happy*. Because I loved her so much, I sought to understand, I wanted to comprehend this most spiritual attainment to the secret of life. I would hug her, look into her eyes, and think to her, "Rumer, show me the way. How, how, can you be so happy. It's so hard for *me*, watching the one I love suffer so. How can you attain such peace?"

And, she showed me, my Angel illuminated the way with the brilliance of an arrow shot straight from Heaven. Her happiness was due to everything that she had in the present, right now. Her life was so full of love, so full of such exquisite beauty because of all she had, all we meant to her, and she to us, that she was fulfilled. With this knowledge, I was freed to savor every moment of my life with her.

On November 26, 2003, Cheryl called Dr. John to talk to him about Rumer's increasingly worrisome condition. He agreed to meet Cheryl and Diane at our house after his rounds that afternoon to check on her. I wasn't yet home from work but was anxiously awaiting Cheryl's call.

Our conversation is still so clear to me when Cheryl called that day after Dr. John left. I was sitting at my desk at work listening so intently to words I did not want to hear. Cheryl said to me, "Well, I just want to let you know what Dr. John said."

For a minute, I perked up, hopeful. Cheryl sounded so upbeat. I soon found that my hope was misplaced—Cheryl's tone was just her way of handling the news. "It's what we thought," she said. "Dr. John thinks that she has six months, until spring at the most."

As Cheryl said these words to me, I suddenly found myself thinking back to the discussion we had with Dr. John a few months previously, a discussion over options for Rumer if her tumors turned malignant. I remembered his words to us, as if I were standing in front of him right now, "In my professional, and personal, opinion, treatments such as chemotherapy just aren't there yet. They might prolong life, but that quality of life is questionable. If she were my dog, I wouldn't put her through such treatments."

Cheryl and I had nodded our heads in agreement, knowing it wouldn't be fair to Rumer to put her through such treatments and make her suffer more. Although I agreed at the time, I also remember stubbornly thinking, "Oh, this is so far off. I won't have to think about her tumors being malignant for ages."

"...so we don't...Are you okay?" Cheryl's voice snapped me back to the horrible present.

I of course answered, "Yes, I'm all right. How's Diane?"

Cheryl said, "Well, she's taking it very hard. She started crying a little when Dr. John told us. She's out there now, playing with Rumer by the pond."

I said, "Okay, I'll see you soon then," barely getting the words out as I started choking up with grief. As soon as I hung up the phone, I quickly went to the restroom at work, where I couldn't help the outburst of sobbing and tears that I could finally let go without audience. I looked at myself in the mirror, tears that I couldn't stop running down my face, and whispered to my reflection, "What am I going to do now, Rumer?" I had not one answer, not one kind, mind-easing response to give back to the grief-stricken reflection that had asked the question so desperately. I reached the end of the road.

When I returned home that Friday night, I read Dr. John's checkup and diagnosis of Rumer, the receipt stating:

- walking (running?) well but circumducts rt. hind leg
- 5 cm thick mamm.on rt hind spread to medial inguinal nodes
- Diagnosis: local invasive adenocarcinoma
- Keep on prednisone
- Try to get to 10 to 20 mg every other day

Seeing it for myself made it all too real. Our minds are so savvy at tricking ourselves, maybe "knowing" something, but not really "knowing" until literally told, a technicality we grasp with the desperation of one grasping at a saving rope when drowning. I was aware of what the tumors meant, but seeing it in writing made me acknowledge the horrible truth. It was a life-changing day for me. I was shattered.

CHAPTER 40

As the brilliant colors of fall gave way to the muted, dying browns and tans of late November and early December, Rumer was less and less mobile. Rob, always the one to shop for her meals and make sure she had the best, knew he was going to have to do some serious research of his own on holistic remedies. He teamed up with Cheryl, both determined to research cancer in dogs and what might help Rumer live a longer, less painful life and boost her immune system. In their research, they found that spirulina consistently appeared in cancer research.

Spirulina is an amazing green algae known to fight radiations and cancers, boost immune systems, and help a variety of ailments. After reading about it extensively, we gave this to Rumer in every meal and, it being a smelly algae powder, she loved it! Rob also found what is known as RM10. It is a very expensive mixture made up of ten different kinds of organic mushrooms that boost the immune system and help fight illnesses such as cancer. He made sure to always keep a supply on hand with his own funds, putting it in every meal for Rumer, along with her spirulina.

In the meantime, Lee was busy doing her own research for her Love. Lee has always been drawn to alternative remedies and philosophies and reads authors such as Linda Goodman. In reading Goodman's books, she learned about something called the "purple plate," a small aluminum plate that is supposed to contain healing properties. She immediately ordered one for Rumer.

As soon as the plate arrived, we placed it on Rumer as often as possible. Whether she was lying on the couch or floor or sleeping in bed, we balanced it on her body. We even put her food and water on the plate for 5 minutes before she ate or drank in order to pass along its healing properties. She accepted this with the patience of a saint, one of us always following her around, plopping this strange purple plate on her, and never questioned what we were doing. Oftentimes, we touched the plate as it rested on Rumer, finding it red-hot, seemingly a sign that it was doing its healing work on the body it touched, taking the heat of cancer into itself.

Although it turned out to be too late to reverse Rumer's rampant cancer, I believe that all of these attempts and holistic treatments did help add another 9 months to her life. It was 9 months more that we had her, 9 months more she blessed our lives, 9 months more of my life as I knew it.

CHAPTER 41

As Rumer's illness progressed, I, for some reason, became obsessed with finding her family. I felt the strongest need to find Wade. I believed that in some way this would comfort me. After looking a bit, I found that he wasn't in Amesbury anymore, so where was he now? Where was this big man with his Yankee accent, and was he still breeding pit bulls? Did he still carry on Rumer's lineage? I searched the internet with a great determination to find out.

After many weeks of doggedly searching, I finally tracked down Wade. He was now in Virginia where, yes, he was still breeding pit bulls of Rumer's direct lineage. After all the work I went through to find it, I gratefully looked through his website, slowly savoring old pictures of Steamer, Rumer's father, and Tyson, her brother who Wade had kept, and all their descendants who were presently being bred. Many pictures were posted including all of Rumer's present relatives.

So happy to have found him, I promptly emailed Wade through his website. I explained who I was and sent him a picture of Rumer. I picked a recent picture of her where she was standing in our pond with her beloved tennis ball floating next to her and 9 baby ducks swimming behind her. It was a beautiful picture of her as she looked later in her life.

Wade emailed back very quickly, happy to hear from me and so happy that we loved Rumer so much, that little pudgy vanilla puppy that had dangled from his hand as he passed her to me so long ago. He thanked me, told me that he loved the picture I sent, and said that he would place this picture and the sentence that I had written about Rumer next to her registered name in the American Pit Bull Registry.

Of course, it would be under her registered name of Goodwin's Chilli Pepper.

After finding Rumer's family, I was more at ease and felt a sense of peace. I didn't contact Wade again until Rumer's death, after which he sent back his condolences and kindly shared a story with me of how he had just lost one of his favorite dogs, Babe, and so understood my pain. Unfortunately, I didn't return to his website for two more years. In 2005 when I did, I was completely shocked to see that he had passed away. At 39 years old, he was killed when a car he was working on fell on him. His website stated that he had, at least, been surrounded by his beloved pit bulls.

Cold weather, slanted, dim rays of the sun pushing through cloudy, raw skies, a halo to the world, I began to hate the passage of time. Along with its cold, winter brought increased pain for Rumer, the Rimadyl not enough anymore. Another call to Dr. John…

…I was finding that, with every new call to Dr. John, my voice changed, became lower, huskier, tearful. This seemed to become an automatic response to hearing his voice, what the call implied, the impending doom.

Rumer was switched to Deramaxx and her dose of prednisone was increased. While helping with her pain, the increased dosage of prednisone brought with it its own set of problems, the worse being the breakdown of her body. A horrible cycle began for Rumer and lasted to the end of her life. The prednisone caused Rumer's immune system to deteriorate. Cheryl and I notified Dr. John, who prescribed a course of antibiotics in order to heal the ensuing sores. The cycle came back every month or so: awful, weeping, open sores all over her body, hair loss, the swelling of her body and weight gain, her thermostat gone haywire causing her to be overheated all the time. Then, a dose of antibiotics, after which she was okay for a month or so until the cycle began again.

When the sores appeared, Cheryl's healing nurse's hands provided comfort to Rumer. Cheryl's touch was so soft, loving, and gentle, "the hands of God" as we often joked. During these horrible periods, Cheryl and I cleaned Rumer's sores every morning and evening. She was so good and so patient in all of her bloated, tumor-ridden pain as we asked her to sit or to lie down on her side. In sitting, she had to sit sideways due to the large tumor in her left groin area. I assisted and comforted Rumer while Cheryl first cleaned her sores with a saline solution and gauze. Next, she tenderly applied triple antibiotic ointment on each and every sore, carefully wiping off the excess so it wouldn't melt on Rumer's overheated body and drip down her sides to cause her discomfort.

As one who was once so proud, healthy, and strong, Rumer bore this all with as much dignity she could muster. She dutifully sat still in order for us to administer to her, so trusting as always in what we were doing, holding such faith and intuitive knowledge that we were helping. As the antibiotics did their work, the few months break from the sores allowed Rumer's body to somewhat heal although dark, hairless patches of these recently healed sores still littered her body.

Throughout this process, this indignity and utter dishonor to this beautiful soul, Rumer taught us over and over the true meaning of being brave and strong, of perseverance in the face of pain and in the knowledge of her own impending death. Cheryl and I became so much closer, bonded by the heaviness of this knowledge in our hearts and loving each other so much more for the care we gently administered to her. Neither one of us ever complained, fought, became tired, or even had to ask each other to help. Even though we were fatigued with her care, and even more so, our grief, we quietly and dutifully went on sharing the administering of Rumer, with utmost love.

It was so hard, though, as she was our family member. It was as if we were watching a sister, a daughter, a niece, or granddaughter suffering, all of those trips to the doctor, to the emergency room, having to give her pills... my whole family came together to help her, but, as in every other life situation, *she* proved the warrior, the teacher, the courageous and patient one.

I... I refused to dwell on all of this. I became so used to her sores, so used to her tumors, so used to her once-beautiful body now bloated, contorting her features until she looked so unlike the Rumer we knew. But, I accepted this because this was who she was now.

I found that my love for Rumer narrowed my life down to the very simple, the whole of my happiness now based on what Rumer could or could not do. I was so happy if I saw the smallest hint of normalcy from her: Rumer in the pond, Rumer riding the cart, Rumer lying in front of the horse fence, hearing Rumer gleefully barking at Grammie's, seeing Rumer's beloved silhouette in the sunset as she limped along with Lee,

Diane, or Grammie in the cooling fall garden. I was overly ecstatic to see anything more from her, maybe a scramble to make it onto the couch herself, hitching herself up our porch stairs to get into the house on her own…that made my day a good day, a fantastic day.

On the other hand, I found myself very depressed if Rumer had a setback: new sores, another tumor, more moles, a day where she couldn't do more than get from point A to point B. These were bad days for me. In looking back at pictures of her during this time, it is painful to imagine how she must have felt.

That fall and winter, even into the blooming of a new spring, Rumer still tried to keep up with her old habits. We all made her life as normal as possible and adjusted our play and activities with her in order for her to be able to do what she wanted. Lee carried her into my parents' basement in order for her to play her beloved hockey. If she was too sore for this, we played a simpler game. She lay on the rug in the living room, facing one of us, as we rolled her tennis ball to her between her front legs. She stopped it with her mouth and flung it back to us with great precision. She loved this and was always so happy, as long as she was still the center of our attention.

She still made her way to Grammie's every morning, with me as her co-pilot, and through the fields back home at night with Lee and Diane. It was at a much slower pace and with more sniffing and resting along the way, but she limped-along home. I still see it all, Lee and Diane in their fall/spring coats, a beautiful chill evening just turning dusk, Rumer waddling along with them on her way home across the fields and over the small brook, her "flying nun" ears silhouetted in the setting sun. I stood on my back deck to watch them making their way, turning my face to the slight breeze with its lingering chill of a winter that didn't want to give in, soaking in the sounds of the night, the peepers in the pond, just beginning their deafening noise, the grasses bent and weaving submissively. As the threesome drew even with the pond, the peepers stopped and quiet descended as the alien footsteps approached. And, as the three continued now past the pond, the peepers started up again once the footsteps faded, happy to fill the night with their music.

I stood there and waited, ready to greet my Rumer as she finally made it home, hold and kiss her head, and ask, "Did you have a good day at Grammie's, Ru?" She covered my face with kisses as I leaned toward her, joyful to see me again.

She still kept Cesa in the horse fence and monitored all horse activities, only not all day like she used to, but rather in bits and spurts. Every six weeks or so, Alan my farrier came to trim the horses' hooves. He pulled into the yard in his Dodge diesel truck, backed up to the barn, and shut the engine with a sputter and large puff of black smoke.

Horse hooves, especially what is called the frog, the spongy, triangular-shaped area under the horse's foot, are a delicacy to most dogs. Rumer just could not resist these trimmings. From my parents' house, she saw Alan's truck pull up to the barn. Soon after, Alan and I heard it, the barking off in the distance as Rumer made her way to us. She came across the fields "whoof...whoof...whoofing" the whole way.

When she finally reached the barn, Alan said, "Hello, Grumpy," as he threw her some hoof.

Never accepting treats or food of any kind from anyone but family, Rumer looked at him sideways, woofing with distrust, and tried to hold out as long as she could. It was just too much for her, though, the smell a maddening attraction. She took the hoof grudgingly, turned, and went to a comfortable, grassy area to enjoy her treat, watching Alan suspiciously the whole time. It was as if he should be honored that she accepted his offering.

When Alan finished shoeing the horses, he left for his next appointment, starting his engine with another sputter and puff of black smoke, rumbling off to Rumer's barking and my waving amidst the smoke and dust. No matter how hard it was for her, Rumer made sure she was with me for these important activities.

And, she still tried to keep up with her usual routines and chores. She was helped onto her golf cart, the Number 8, and lolled on the seat all day, her driver taking her around the property... She was made a part of everything, totally expecting to be, our methods of doing something determined by her. If she told us she could walk, we walked, if she couldn't, she was helped onto the cart and driven. There was nothing to think about; it's just how it was done.

As Rumer's tumors continued to grow, she found it harder and harder to walk on floors without carpeting. Our house has many rooms with wood and tile flooring which worried Cheryl and me. We were so afraid that Rumer might fall or break a leg that we purchased throw rugs to scatter along these slippery floors. She knew what these rugs were meant for, carefully avoiding the slippery areas and staying on the traction, planning her route by how the carpets were arranged.

Late winter/early spring brought an additional medication, torbutrol, which is an opiate pain reliever. Rumer was so bloated from her medications and insatiable appetite that her usual 75-80 pounds jumped to a whopping 92. She wanted to eat all the time and begged shamefully, especially taking a liking to sweets.

With her new size, however, came another problem. She was much too heavy for me to carry upstairs to bed. Since I am only 5 feet tall and weigh about 25 pounds more than this, I found myself completely unable to conquer this problem, my determination to get us all to our haven outweighed, literally, by the reality of our situation. The easier solution for Cheryl and me was that we'd move our bedroom, our haven, to her.

One unusually warm late winter weekend, Cheryl and I, with my family's help, moved from upstairs into the downstairs guest bedroom. With fans going and windows open to the first fresh air of approaching spring, we all felt enthusiastic and hopeful, accomplishing something new for Rumer.

Throughout Rumer's and Lily's whole lives, we *always* slept in our bedroom upstairs. But, once we moved to the first floor, it felt good and right, both Rumer and Lily taking this big change in perfect stride. Into the guest room we all moved, maybe different surroundings but the aura of love and comfort among the occupants the same. Rumer was happy with the new arrangements because she could easily get to the bedroom again on her own, which had the additional bonus of carpeting! Of course, her dog ramp came with us, parked on the edge of the bed, up which we guided Rumer every night. Lily loved the ease of our new surroundings, too, and made use of the dog ramp herself. She also developed arthritis, which interfered with her jumping abilities, and used the ramp with great appreciation.

The return of "my" swallows, the screeching of the jays, the horses shedding out their thick winter coats for ones of sleek, soft velvet, the warm, healing rays of the sun, the passing of time moving much too quickly into the spring of 2004… Rumer was now just so hot all of the time. She was always panting, her body a swollen, burning mass. We ran a window fan, the ceiling fan, and a stand-up oscillating fan all night to combat some of her discomfort. I took nice soft cloths, ran them under cool water, and brought them to the bed where Rumer lay to squeeze them out over her head and ears and lovingly wipe her whole face with the coolness. Though it helped to cool her, she hated this. She saw me coming, dripping cloth in my hand, and gave me that sideways look, dipping her head in displeasure yet bearing it all the same because she knew it brought her some relief.

As Rumer's condition worsened, Cheryl changed her hours at work for three of the five days a week so that the two of us could commute. The walk to Grammie's finally became too difficult for her, so Cheryl and I drove Rumer up to Grammie's every morning on our way to work together. Previously hating to travel in the car, Rumer acquiesced to the drive since it now meant getting her to Grammie's. Once there, I lifted Rumer gently down to the house entryway. Rumer, even in her excitement to get into Grammie's house and greet everyone on this wonderful new day, paused. She looked back and waited, gazing at me intently with her almond-shaped eyes.

"Have a good day at Grammie's, Ru. I love you," I told her as I took her head in my hands and kissed her now-white mush.

This did the usual trick of freeing her. Standing there, I watched her go, watched her limping body, her back legs spread by tumors, as she made her way into Grammie's open front door, my heart breaking. It took all I could not to run to help her, to kneel on the cement in front of her and hug her into infinity. Hearing the usual enthusiastic greetings of my family as she entered the house helped my heart, helped me gain the strength to turn away and leave.

My family, as well, adjusted to Rumer's needs, especially at this point when she couldn't make long walks anymore. Diane and Lee drove her back home at night in Diane's car or, if it was a warmer evening, on her beloved golf cart. Her golf cart, Number 8, was now the staple for traveling the yard. It became her wheelchair, her literal lifesaver. Number 8 was good to Rumer and really the only way she was able to go on as long as she did. It became her sole method of mobility. Since she had grown up being driven around on the golf cart, this means of transportation for her now was not an affront to her dignity, was not really a reminder of her lack of mobility or health.

At the same time Rumer's lack of mobility increased, Diane lost her full-time job. Since she found a part-time job to replace it, this allowed her to make up her own hours. It also enabled her to spend time with Rumer at the exact moment Rumer needed her most. She gave Rumer the care that she needed and kept Rumer company in her last days. She loved Rumer so much that she adjusted her life in order to accommodate Rumer's needs. This is when she and Rumer became the best of buddies. Diane drove Rumer around on the golf cart daily, bringing her wherever they needed to go. Sometimes, Diane drove to… just drive. As she said to Rumer, "Let's put the pedal to the metal, Rumer, and make your ears fly."

Especially on hotter days when Rumer needed to cool off, Diane drove full blast. The two of them laughed, Diane out loud and Rumer in her pit bull way, head up, mouth open wide in a panting grin, ears flapping. I watched them fly around the property, hitting bumps here and there, throwing them around on the cart seat, making them laugh even more. I loved this sight so much, the sound of the electric cart mixing with Diane's joyful laugh.

As Rumer continued on into the late spring of 2004, I held my breath as the six-month deadline for her demise came and went. She continued on, happily limping along. Rumer's obsession with food proved a good thing by then. She ate anything we gave her, even a piece of lettuce from our salads flavored with bitter dressings. She was on so many pills by this time and we easily hid them in food—any kind of food. This stayed the same until the very end, too, with Rumer eating a chicken breakfast (off of a fork of course) the morning of her death.

CHAPTER 42

I released a shaky, long-held breath as Rumer passed the sixth month point, only to have another circumstance blindside us all. My mother was sent for medical tests that May since she hadn't been feeling well for a while. After numerous appointments, the tests eventually revealed a blockage in the neck artery leading to her brain and blockages in her heart arteries as well.

The doctors attacked my mother's heart problem first by performing an angioplasty. This procedure allows the doctors to enter the groin artery and travel up to the heart in order to place stents in the heart arteries, opening up the blocked areas. On the day of the procedure, Cheryl and I, along with my whole family, sat in the hospital waiting room anxiously awaiting the result.

When the doctor finally came out to speak with us, he brought us to a quiet waiting room and asked us all to sit down. I felt myself becoming numb as, head down, not meeting our eyes, he told us that the procedure had been unsuccessful. My mother's blockages were just too far along to fix by this most noninvasive method. He told us, "She's been dodging bullets for quite a while and we're lucky nothing worse has happened to her so far. But, we need to correct her problems immediately."

The bottom line: it was imperative that she have open-heart surgery as well as an endarterectomy, surgery on her neck artery, which proved even more dangerous than the heart surgery.

The day of my mother's operation and the following weeks were a horrible blur. The actual morning of her surgery, my whole family sat in the hospital waiting room again and waited all afternoon into early evening. At 10:30 that evening, the heart surgeon came to notify us that my mother had gotten through everything just fine. We soon learned, though, that this proved just the beginning of a long, painful, and difficult road to recovery that lay ahead for her. From May onward, my mother and Rumer spent every day together, my mother recovering and Rumer deteriorating, but both serving as such a great comfort and help to each other.

The rest of us began a delicate juggling act of caring for both my mother and Rumer. Lee's bosses, Dr. Joe and Dr. Kay, bless both their hearts, allowed Lee to change her work schedule and cut her hours... Diane, still working part-time...all of us pitching in any way we could to help care for our two loves.

Cheryl and I were so grateful for my family's help during this difficult time. While caring for my mother, everyone was also entrusted with Rumer's hospice care, trusted to give her medications, to clean sores, to attend to her needs, which they did as selflessly as Cheryl and I. We could never have done it all for Rumer without them.

June 2004 was proving to be the beginning of a brutally hot summer. My agitation and worry for Rumer increased tenfold. Heat, never Rumer's friend, both demolished and depleted her more than anything else in her illness. This hot, dry summer sucked away the remaining reserves she had. My family was even more diligent in her care. They brought her into air conditioning often. When outside, they placed a baseball hat and sun glasses on her and made sure to park her in the shade when on the golf cart or under a canopy when by the pool. Diane even cut the edges of Rumer's baseball cap so that they came down protectively to cover Rumer's ears. The gnats were just as ferocious as the heat and ate Rumer's ears mercilessly.

I think that at this time, Rumer's many medications and illness affected her more than we wanted to realize. One very hot evening that June, as Cheryl and I watched TV, I noticed Rumer begin to act very antsy. I thought she just had to potty, so I called her to the front door and let her out. It was pitch black, 10:00 in the evening, the peepers at full volume, the front floodlights the only illumination. I watched closely through the front window but lost sight of her as she left the haloed edge of light. I waited a few minutes, but Rumer didn't return.

I yanked open the front door and called to her—no Rumer. I

quickly put on my sneakers, got a flashlight, and ran out to the front yard—no Rumer anywhere. I ran back into the house yelling to Cheryl in a panic, "Can you come help me? Rumer's missing!"

Cheryl came running while yelling, "What do you mean missing?!"

We both ran back outside, calling and searching, to no avail. Without knowing what else to do, we hurried back in the house and called my family. When they answered, trying to calm my voice, I asked, "Do you guys happen to see Rumer up there? I let her out and can't find her—she hasn't come back."

I heard everyone yelling at once in the background, the scruffing of running feet, the yell of my sisters as they saw Rumer outside their front door, the sigh of relief from me that Rumer was there.

"She's here! We have her!" my sisters yelled into the phone.

Although relieved, my heart broke a little at this new development. Was Rumer confused, was she in pain, did she need the comfort of my family more than Cheryl and me?

Cheryl and I jumped into the car and raced to my parents' house. We went in the front door and saw our Rumer, in her spot on their couch, looking at us and laughing in her panting way. Her tail thumped a greeting as she looked at us as though this was the most normal thing, limping to Grammie's alone, in total darkness. Cheryl and I ran to her and hugged her, one of us on each side, both of us saying, "Let's go home now, Rumer, okay?"

And we did, lifting Rumer off the couch, helping her out the front door and putting her into the car. Once back in bed, she settled in and seemed okay as she quickly fell into a sound sleep. Slowly, muscle by muscle, I felt the tension in my body ease as I listened to the most wonderful sound in the world, her soft snoring.

CHAPTER 43

Mid-June brought an unforeseen incident that depleted Rumer's waning energy even more. Rumer had developed a few skin tags on different parts of her body. Skin tags are long pieces of limp skin that grow out and hang from the normal skin. One of her skin tags grew out of her belly and became quite long. As it grew, Cheryl and I worried that it might get caught on something and cause a problem.

Nobody saw it happen, but happen it did one very hot and humid Friday evening. The Thursday night before, we had spent the night in the hospital when my mother experienced a sudden spike in her blood pressure. Everything turned out okay but, now, the very next evening, Rumer's skin tag had somehow ripped away from her belly, causing an eruption of blood. She desperately needed medical help herself.

It was almost 8:00 Friday evening. We called Dr. John only to find that he was away on vacation. Panic struck as Cheryl and I, my sisters, and my parents frantically discussed where to take Rumer without having to subject her to a 40 minute drive to the nearest 24-hour emergency animal hospital. The blood was just torrential and we were using everything from sanitary pads to towels to staunch the flow. Cheryl finally called an animal hospital about 10 minutes from our house, the only problem was that they closed at 8:00. Probably due to her shameless pleading, the receptionist, after asking the resident doctor, came back to the phone and said to Cheryl, "The doctor said she'd wait for you. Just come right away."

Scurrying Rumer along, Cheryl, Diane, Lee, and I ran to my Toyota Corolla. We lifted Rumer into the back seat between Lee and Diane, my mother and father worriedly watching and waving from the driveway. We left so fast that we forgot a collar for Rumer. We didn't even have a leash. Too late to turn back, I drove, Cheryl directed me where to go, and my sisters sat in the back seat with Rumer, trying to hold pressure on her belly. Rumer's howls echoed in the car, a voice of displeasure as we sped out of the yard.

We reached the hospital after ten long minutes and gently led Rumer to the waiting vet tech and resident vet. They quickly ushered us into an extremely hot exam room. When the door was shut, it seemed as though the air just whooshed out, and it became unbearably stifling with the four of us taking up every square inch of the room. I kneeled to help pin Rumer to the floor and felt sweat dripping down my back, soaking my shirt. Rumer, panting, trying to catch the slight breeze that wafted in through the small crack along the bottom of the shut door, lay on her heaving side while the doctor checked her bleeding stomach.

After a torturously long exam and discussion of what to do, the vet finally admitted that she didn't know how to stitch Rumer's stomach properly. "Let's try putting a 'sock' around her stomach. That should hold until Dr. John returns. Then he can stitch it for you," she told us.

I just knew the sock wouldn't hold. I knew that this piece of gauze that slipped over Rumer's middle area wasn't capable of staunching the flow of blood that was coming from her. But, I was willing to give it a try. The doctor had been so nice to wait for us, and, I just prayed I would be wrong.

While I stayed to pay, Diane, Lee, and Cheryl took Rumer to the car to wait. I was writing out the check when Cheryl came running back in, "It didn't work—she started bleeding all over again!"

We now knew there was no choice but to make the 40 minute trip to Springfield where the 24-hour emergency clinic was located. "We'll call ahead to let them know you're coming," the receptionist told me as I quickly added a leash to the bill, and off we flew to Springfield.

Dusk turned to darkness as we drove. By the time we reached the emergency clinic, it was pitch dark. Rumer had quieted through the drive, calmly sitting between her aunts, but when we pulled into the parking lot, poor Rumer...once again, we dragged her out of the car and through the dimly-lit entryway of the clinic. Gently as we could, Cheryl and I led the bleeding Rumer with a looped nylon leash we had just purchased while my sisters walked crouched over, trying to keep pressure on her stomach with sanitary pads.

There was so much brightness as we entered the hospital, blinding lights, busy, milling people and animals in the waiting area, everyone making way as they saw us coming. "Triage! Triage!" yelled a vet tech as, alerted from our previous stop, she ran to meet us.

In the middle of it all came Rumer, back left leg out at an angle, body swollen with tumors, spilling blood all over their floor as we approached. The vet tech tried to take her from us, telling us we couldn't come, but Cheryl yelled, "We're not leaving her! She's dying of cancer and is under our hospice care and we won't leave her alone!" to which a sympathetic outburst of "ohhhhh"s and "nooooo"s erupted from the waiting people.

Diane and I walked zombie-like to the counter to pay the emergency fee, trusting Cheryl and Lee to go with Rumer while the vet took her into the back room. Worried and quiet, I waited for my receipt at the counter. As I turned toward Diane, I saw Cheryl and Lee coming back out of the check-up room, one thing terribly wrong: they were without Rumer. They walked toward us, Cheryl muttering and sputtering while Lee patiently listened, head cocked toward Cheryl. We all met in the waiting area as Diane and I whispered frantically to them, "Where's Rumer?"

Cheryl said, "They wouldn't let us stay with her so I told them to 'just do what you have to do then and hurry up!'"

Diane and I incredulously exclaimed at the same time, "You left her alone?!"

This caused an eruption of argued whispering among the four of us. We continued to argue about who was going to go back into the exam room if Rumer wasn't returned soon. Eventually, we wore both each other and ourselves out. Dehydrated and sick, we watched as the vet tech mopped Rumer's blood from the slippery waiting room floor, getting sympathetic glances from those waiting along with us.

After a painfully long 30 minutes, the door opened to one of the rooms and out burst Rumer, energetically leading the vet who had worked on her. She was bright-eyed, happy, flying-nun ears in their perked position. The blood was cleaned off of her and she was eagerly pulling to get to us, looking so much okay! The vet explained to Cheryl how she had stitched Rumer's wound and said, "That should hold for now, but, Dr. John should probably reinforce it when he returns. It's in a bad, vulnerable spot."

We thanked her profusely as Lee and Diane led Rumer out to the car, Rumer pulling madly to get out of that place. Cheryl and I ran to join them and we began the 40 minute drive home, Rumer now much happier.

Rumer really seemed no worse for the wear. I was surprised at how well she actually took the trauma. She went right into an exhausted sleep when we got home and was raring to go and happy the next day upon waking. We all had a fantastic, busy weekend. I thought the experience would've depleted her for days, but she actually seemed better than she had been in a long time. I was so encouraged and enthusiastic about this, a false hope, I learned, in the bumpy road of her illness.

With Rumer softly snoring in bed, Cheryl and I talking, even laughing in hysterical relief about the experience we just had, I was just so happy she was here, with us, with me. Having her back home that night only proved a stay of the eventual life I would have to live without her, but it was a stay I appreciated and savored, holding on to it as gently and reverently as the most fragile-winged butterfly.

Wednesday evening the next week, the four of us brought Rumer to Dr. John's office in Holyoke to have her skin tag re-stitched. This office visit actually proved to take more out of Rumer than the Friday night before. As was the whole summer, it was a brutally hot early evening as we waited to be seen, sitting in an extremely sweltering waiting room. Rumer stared unseeingly and inconsolably out the window at the streets below, emitting her "harrr" the whole time. Once in the examining room, my face round with shock and grief, Rumer demurely allowed Dr. John to re-stitch her wound. We left, Lee and Diane helping us, once again, bring Rumer down the stairs and back into the car. Cheryl and I knew immediately that Rumer wasn't right. She was more tired than ever before.

The next week, the week of June 29th, back came the sores. After calling Dr. John that Saturday, Cheryl and I drove to his clinic to pick up more antibiotics, Cephalexin and Orbax. It was during this visit that we broached the subject with him about options for Rumer's body after she passed. In his office, where he was nice enough to meet us even though the clinic was closed, we spoke in hushed tones while he prepared the prescriptions and I watched the muted, peaceful sunlight streaming through the shades of his beautiful Victorian clinic. I so much wanted to avoid the discussion we were having, and would much rather just enjoy the peace of the moment. As I forced myself to participate and listen, Dr. John was explaining the option of cremation. He wrote down the person he recommended if we decided to do this, sadly handing over the note and the now-ready prescriptions.

We left Dr. John that morning with much to think about, appreciative of his patience and kindness in the midst of something so difficult. I couldn't cry... where were the tears when we had just spoken about the very thing that would eventually crush me? How could I just talk about cremating the body that I revered, that I so needed to touch, to hug, the brown eyes that looked back into my own with such understanding and knowledge, the tongue that kissed me with such passion and unconditional love? How could we have so calmly discussed this? Having always had to be strong and show I could take everything in stride, I thought, "If I start crying, I don't think I'll ever be able to stop. I'll just collapse in a sobbing heap around whom everyone will have to walk in order to go about their lives."

As often as schedules permit, Cheryl and I have her sister Wendy and our niece Selena stay for the weekend to visit. I'll never forget when they came to our house on one of the last weekends Rumer was still with us. Cheryl and I threw open the front door to their welcome presence, hugging and kissing them in greeting. As Wendy came into the living room, she was greeted by a laughing, licking Rumer. She looked down to pet Rumer in welcome too, and as her eyes came to rest upon Rumer, all she said was, "Oh my God, Jolene..."

Since we all saw Rumer every day and cared for her declining body, it didn't matter how she looked. She was our Rumer, our eternally beautiful daughter, granddaughter, niece. It was only through Wendy's eyes that day that I really *saw* how shocking Rumer's condition had become.

Those four simple words spoke volumes.

CHAPTER 44

Escalating with the heat of the summer was the decline of Rumer's health. She was tired, sick, in pain, and oh-so-hot during this brutal season. We all made sure to wet her head and body down with cool, soaked cloths, like a dolphin out of water. I worried so much during these hot summer days in which even the breezes that appeared were hot that Rumer would actually die from the heat either by getting heat stroke or just giving in to death. Diane was now the one caring for her the most. She could hardly do anything else any more. Rumer now needed constant vigilance, constant attention.

The pretending, the denial of how serious her illness was—it was all over. We all silently knew there was little time left. Cheryl and I found that we did not want to leave Rumer any more than was necessary. In the past, we'd occasionally go out to eat with friends or with family, make day trips, or go shopping. But now, we both had a silent agreement to stay home during any and all of our spare time. My family felt the same way, Lee racing home from work every night, my mother forgoing shopping, nobody suggesting going out to eat. The unspoken agreement with us all: Rumer must not be left alone for any amount of time…

…of most importance, we didn't want anything else in life to take away one second of the time we had left with her.

My love, my sweet Angel Pie, my companion, my teacher, my nurse. How I wish I could take away your pain, take it within myself to bear for you, as you always did for me. The only help I can give you is to take from my needs, to become selfless and unconditionally giving. For, I can't hold you any more at night or spoon you for my own comfort—you can't stand the heat of my touch. Even the feather-light touch of my hand on you is too much, the pressure on your body, the heat on already overheated skin. My hand still crawls forward of its own accord, unstoppable, seeking your sleeping body, missing so grievously its source of peace and comfort and strength. And, I certainly can't reveal the hurt that consumes my heart, my total and intense grief. For, you need my strength now, you need to know from me that all is well, though it isn't. I find that my love for you is so great, so complete, so pure that I can, once again, forgo anything in order to allow you what you need for your remaining time with me.

FINAL

My angel from heaven. You have gone from being my rock of strength in body and soul to my rock of strength in soul only. Your heavy body has betrayed you, has proven to hold back the spirit within you that is still as free and as light as an angel's wings. I cradle your now-swollen body so gently, for it is rugged and strong no more. I touch you and hold you so carefully, like glass that threatens to shatter at any moment. You need our care though you still ask for nothing. I know that you try not to be a burden so that you can stay with us forever—but, did I ever tell you that nothing that you could ever need in the world could ever be a burden?

How I wish your body could be as free as your spirit once more.

CHAPTER 45

The sleepless nights began in September 2004. The sleeplessness, the staring, the whining due to I'm not sure what...discomfort? Pain? Confusion?

Cheryl and I tried all our tricks: telling her to settle, softly rubbing the insides of her forearms. We were in the downstairs bedroom, three fans going for her comfort, Lily always joining us on the bed since she loved Rumer so much too, braving the wind from the fans that she hated in order to be with us. It seemed as if all of this were in vain, though, all the comfort, all the love—none of this seemed to help Rumer anymore.

Of everything that had happened, everything we'd been through over the course of Rumer's illness, the pills, the sores, the tumors, the incapacitation, this was the most disturbing development to me. This had been the one constant throughout everything in life, Rumer's soft snoring, her slow, peaceful breathing, always able to put Cheryl and me to sleep no matter how stressed or upset we were. I think I related the whole of her illness, of how she was feeling, to her sleep pattern. If Rumer could sleep, she was okay and I could rest easy.

This sleeplessness, this looking at us and whining, made me sick inside. It devastated me and filled me with desolation and profound fatigue. I just wish I could understand. Was she asking us to help her? Was this the end?

After a few nights, Cheryl and I were exhausted with worry and lack of sleep. We contacted Dr. John about this new development. After listening, he told us to come pick up some Diazepam, which is a type of valium, to help this restlessness. That first week in September, we picked up three prescriptions: Cephalexin, Torbutrol, and the Diazepam. She was now on at least five medications daily. As a precaution, Dr. John also prescribed torbugesic, a potent form of morphine. "Just in case you need it," he said. Have I said enough how much I love this man, another angel sent to us in our time of need?

Unfortunately, the Diazepam helped for only a short amount of time. By September 14th, after a week or so of reprieve, Rumer again was inconsolable at night. I called Dr. John late that Wednesday night, after Cheryl and I realized we were through with all options. I tried so hard not to cry, to control my quavering voice, as I told him how Rumer was, again having a difficult time. Dr. John, with all the sympathy and gentleness he could convey in his voice told me, "Well, give her one morphine for the night and again in the morning if she needs more. Let me know how everything goes."

As soon as I hung up with Dr. John, I called my family to tell them about Rumer's condition. No one really said anything—what could we say?—all of us cocooned in our own anguish. Cheryl and I had a vacation planned for the next week and were living for that time, so hopeful that it would be time together with Rumer, to catch up on sleep, to maybe heal a little, to have just another week!

But, it wasn't to be. The next morning, Thursday, Rumer was no better. Cheryl gave her more morphine and, finally acknowledging that Rumer would never be getting better, called out sick from work, feeling a great need to stay home with her.

I rose that morning, so exhausted myself. I scuffed into the kitchen to make the coffee and glanced out the window to a beautiful fall morning as I ran the water into the pot. I stood, absently gazing out at the horses, Cesa looking in the window at me, anxiously awaiting her breakfast, and saw Diane walking by the house. Head down, arms hugging herself, she was crying, not wanting to bother us, but wanting to see Rumer so desperately. I yelled this to Cheryl, so broken up to see Diane in this condition. Cheryl, upset for Diane too, ran to the front door and called out to her, "Come in and see her! She's okay right now."

Diane, in all her grief, came quickly into the bedroom to see Rumer, smiling in joy at Rumer's laughing greeting from the bed, falling to her knees, hugging and kissing Rumer "good morning." There was no denying the love that Rumer had for Diane. She kissed and kissed Diane all over her face, cleaning her tears. It was hard to tell who was kissing who more. After their enthusiastic greeting, Diane helped Rumer off the bed, down the dog ramp, out the front door, and into the yard.

While Cheryl stayed home with Diane and Rumer that day, I left for work as usual, working 1:00 pm to 9:00 pm on Thursdays. After kissing and hugging Rumer extra long, and telling Cheryl I loved her, too, I left for work though my heart was bursting. I was in a fog for most of the day, not knowing what to do with myself. At 6:30 that evening, Cheryl called me. "Hi, Hon. You need to come home right away. I'm sorry to tell you this, but Rumer's not doing well."

Denying this moment, hoping for a stay, I asked, "Are you sure?"

"Very," she said. "Your mother and sisters are here on the bed with Rumer. We're all talking and holding her, but you need to come home, too, to be with her."

"Okay, I'll be right there," I said numbly.

Then, Cheryl surprised me by adding, "Your mother is going to have a friend call soon to 'speak' to Rumer. She's an animal communicator, so your mother thought we could all ask Rumer some questions and hear what she might have to tell us."

"Oh," I said with a flicker of interest. "Okay, I'll be home as quickly as I can. Love you."

"Love you too, and be careful," Cheryl answered.

After making it home through my torturous 35-minute drive, Cheryl met me alone, without the usual accompaniment of Rumer at the front door. After silently hugging each other tightly for a minute, we both walked into the bedroom, words not necessary. I couldn't meet anyone's eyes as I walked up to my Rumer who was watching my progress from the bed. I bent to kiss her "hello," taking her head in my hands as I'd done so many times.

"Hello, Angel Pie," I said. "Mama's here now."

And, into my eyes Rumer looked while she kissed me and wagged her tail, still giving her all for me. I knelt on the floor next to her on the bed as conversation quietly resumed. I honestly can't even remember the inane things we talked about as we surrounded Rumer that evening. We were just content to be together, savoring every minute we had. We peacefully waited for my mother's friend to call, all of us hoping, I'm sure, to "tell" Rumer everything we wanted her to know, this being the last night on earth we would be spending with her.

At 7:30, the call came. After introducing herself to us on speakerphone, my mother's friend asked to "speak" with Rumer. She then asked to speak to each of us privately in turn, one at a time. And, as she spoke to each of us, she told us what Rumer was trying to communicate. She then asked if we had any questions for Rumer.

The whole scene was completely surreal to me. The lighting was dim, Cheryl, my mother, my two sisters, me—we were all there, surrounding Rumer on the bed, Rumer panting as her head slowly rotated to each of us in turn as we spoke, listening, still in such good humor and so happy we were giving her such absolute attention. As my turn came, I took the phone nervously, placed it to my ear and heard a question, "Would you like me to ask Rumer anything for you?"

"No," I said, "Thank you, but I can't really think of anything at the moment."

"Okay," she answered, "I'll just tell you what she wants you to know."

I listened with such hope, such anticipation for some profound truth that Rumer needed me to know. The communicator started her very first sentence to me, "Rumer is telling me to tell you that she'll be happy when she passes, that she'll finally be able to chase all the squirrels she wants to again."

Devastated, I stopped listening. Though nodding absently now and then as she spoke, as if she could see me, I honestly cannot remember anything else the communicator told me. Rumer never did like to chase squirrels. She thought that this activity was much below her, a very "doglike" thing to do, and nothing to which she'd succumb.

If there was a profound truth to be had from the experience, it was that no one knew Rumer better than we. It revealed, again, the lengths we would go to show how much we loved her, but we should have faith that whatever Rumer had to tell us and us her had already been told throughout our whole lives together. And, maybe this was the whole purpose of the experience, after all.

After finishing with the communicator, I felt it coming off each of us in waves of anxiety as no one wanted this evening to end, an end that would mean so much more than just another wonderful day gone by.

But, at 9:30, my mother and sisters said their 'goodbyes,' hugging and kissing Rumer for at least another fifteen minutes before leaving.

Cheryl, Lily, Rumer, and I then settled in to watch TV, relax, and hopefully, sleep. But, this didn't happen—Rumer could not settle down at all. We had gone through 4 morphine pills and were down to one left. As the night continued with Rumer in distress, Cheryl and I realized what needed to be done. We looked at each other, the weight too much to bear.

"Can you please make the call?" Cheryl finally asked me, tears in her voice.

I couldn't answer. I just picked up the phone and dialed Dr. John's number, knowing it better than my own. I almost couldn't speak when I heard his voice, almost not strong enough after all. But I gathered all the strength I had in my body, delving into my very soul for Rumer and asking Dr. John, "I think it's time, can you please come tomorrow?"

This simple plea was the best I could do.

"Of course I'll come," he said. "I can be there at about 11:30 tomorrow morning."

After gently placing the phone down in its cradle, I couldn't choke back the tears any longer. As the floodtide began, I turned to Cheryl. We hugged each other as tightly as we could and cried, a hand from each of us stroking Rumer's poor body as we clung to each other. Lily sweetly purred at my feet, the four of us an unbreakable circle of love.

CHAPTER 46

Friday, September 17, 2004, was the day that changed everything thereafter for me.

Cheryl and I woke up from very little sleep with, again, an agitated Rumer. We both called out sick from work, then settled in to spend our last moments with our Rumer, wiped out and in shock.

Rumer didn't get up with us, but stayed in bed, head resting on front paws, eyes never stopping in their watchfulness, following our every move. I scuffed into my sneakers and, in a fog, made my way to the barn to feed Cesa. Rob was driving by to go on a brief errand, but stopped to hug and kiss me and ask, "Can I go in to see Rumer quick?"

"Of course, go on in. I'm just going to feed Cesa, but I'll be right there," I answered as I hugged him tightly in return.

I finished in the barn and went back in the house to make my coffee and get Rumer's breakfast ready. Coffee in one hand, her chicken and rice plate in the other, I approached the bedroom where Rob was kneeling beside the bed, kissing Rumer. He said, "I'll be back, Rumer. I just have to go out for a few minutes. But, I'll be back soon."

Rumer's illness never affected her appetite, and as I fed her breakfast with a fork, I desperately hoped it might settle her down in some way, alleviate her agitation just a little. As she took her last forkful, I realized that we were suddenly alone. I heard Cheryl outside the bedroom door talking to Diane, who had just arrived. Rob had left, so it was just me and my Ru facing each other, nothing but raw, open emotions between us.

That morning, that small amount of alone-time with her was the most precious moment I ever shared with her. While I heard the soft murmurings of Diane and Cheryl, I looked at Rumer with every ounce of love in my being. Kneeling on the floor in front of the bed, Rumer lying on the edge listening to me, I held her dear head in my two hands, stared into her eyes, and spoke to her. For the last time, I told her how so very much I loved her, how so very happy she made me, how honored I was to have her in my life and to be her mother, how so proud I was of her, of all that she did and was, how so complete my life was because of her.

Her brown eyes held mine, even through her haze of pain and morphine, as she concentrated on my face, her tail thumping slowly, still wagging. And, I stared back into her beautiful brown almond-shaped eyes surrounded by mascara, as black as it was that wonderful, joyous day we picked her out as a baby, but a muzzle now whitened with age. I searched her face so intently through eyes out of which I could barely see, blinking quickly so as to blink back the tears. I wanted so desperately to etch in my brain forever how she looked and felt and smelled. I scrutinized every mole, every hair, every scar that Lee or I or Cheryl had so lovingly applied zinc ointment to at one time or another to help heal the various cuts and scratches she got throughout her busy life. I tried to relive her whole life story, all our experiences together, all the funny moments, all she was, by staring into her precious face.

My whole world now became this one moment in time, this moment I would have given my life for to last longer, this one small space, a tunnel vision which consisted of her face and blocked out all else. I didn't see her tired cancer-ridden body, the wrists deformed with arthritis, her once beautifully-muscled shape now a swollen blob. I didn't see any of this, just her loving, kind, beautiful, and pure soul looking out at me. I tried so hard not to cry, to be brave and strong one more time for her, in front of her, to give her what she deserved after a lifetime of giving to me selflessly. But, I couldn't stop the tears that came. And, as they flowed, I realized that maybe Rumer didn't mind seeing me cry—a testament to how much she meant to me.

"I love thee so, Angel Pie," I said to her at last as I took my tear-stained face and rubbed it reverently all over her, rubbing my tears into her fur. "With these tears, I will always be with you now, My Love." Rumer kissed me and then placed her heavy, tired head in my hands, staring into my now clear-eyed face as Diane and Cheryl approached.

When Diane entered the room with Cheryl, it was once again clear how much Rumer loved her. She even hoisted herself up on her own and started down the dog ramp to get to her. Out the front door they rushed to potty quickly and then jump onto the golf cart, Number 8. Lee came down soon after and both she and Diane sat with her on the cart, kissing and hugging her. When Rumer started whining in agitation almost immediately, Cheryl gave her the last morphine, after which Diane and Lee drove the golf cart around the yard to help cool her down on this sizzling September morning. Diane and Lee pulled up to our house after a few rounds and asked, "Jo, Cheryl, is it okay if we take Rumer up to Grammie's? It's her usual routine, so might calm her, might help her settle down a little."

"It's okay with us," Cheryl said, "but is it okay with you that Dr. John will have to come to your house, then, to give Rumer her final peace?"

After saying that they'd be honored to have Rumer at their house, Lee and Diane took her to Grammie's and helped her to her place on the couch for some final quiet and rest.

Cheryl and I followed soon after. As we walked up the gravel drive and approached my parents' house, we realized that Rob had come back already, Paul had come, and everyone else was there to be with Rumer. How unbelievably wonderful and what a compliment to her life and what she meant to us all that we were all there for her death. She went to her grave knowing how much she was loved, how so very much she would be missed. In our faces, though wrought with grief, was only the purest reflection of what she was and what she had done for each of us throughout her life. She saw how proud of her we were, proud of how she had risen, without hesitation, to all the challenges that were posed to her, and had so eloquently supported that weight that we had placed upon her shoulders so many years ago as that little red puppy named Chilli Pepper. What a brave and beautiful soul that stared back at us, more brave and kind than anyone I've ever known in my whole life.

Dr. John arrived soon after 11:30 that morning. As he got out of his car and approached my parents' house, Cheryl and I went out to greet him. He came to us, warmly giving us each a hug, and said, "She made it a lot longer than we thought."

I smiled at him for his kindness, blinking through the tears that were in my eyes, trying to see as we made our way to the house, the sun seemingly much too bright. We heard Rumer begin her usual barking at him, seeing him approach through my parents' front bay window. We came in the front door to her incessant barking and she looked at Dr. John from the couch with her sideways look while he exclaimed, "Oh, Rumer, that sound is going to greet me at the gates of Heaven!"

We all gathered in my parents' living room, surrounding Rumer, to listen as Dr. John explained what would happen. He said that he would first give her a shot to relax her and then would come back for her final shot. Without further delay, he walked behind the couch and gave her the first shot in her back thigh. She didn't like this at all, and Lee and Diane had to comfort her, saying, "It's okay, Rumer, it's not a bee…all done." Dr. John left after, stepping out the front door to wait in the yard beyond, while my family spent our last few moments with Rumer.

They say that when it's time, your pet will be grateful for your selfless act of putting them to sleep. They will be ready to go and will finally sigh with relief that the end to their pain and suffering will be allowed them, our own selfishness given up to do what's best for them. They say that you will be able to see the thankfulness in their eyes at your decision for them, absolving you from the guilt of this very difficult decision.

But, I must say that this did not happen with Rumer, nor with my Taja, for that matter. Neither one wanted to go, neither had been ready to leave us yet, Taja fighting the shots to the end. And, with Rumer, if it were up to her, we would all stay like this indefinitely, sitting here in this circle of love, giving her our sole attention, the whole family together into infinity. It made it all so much harder. I looked around the living room, trying to memorize these moments, Rumer's last ones with us, as much as possible, everything like a slide show in my mind:

My mother, so recently out of bypass, Rumer's buddy for the past four months, sitting in her chair by the couch, her recliner on which she and Rumer both napped together. She was weeping the whole time, sobbing, every once in a while exclaiming, "Look at her!" waving her hand, which was clutching a tissue, in Rumer's direction. She was bent over some pieces of paper, frantically writing a letter the whole time. This letter went to Rumer's grave, the contents of which only she and Rumer know. I never saw my mother cry like this in my life.

For some reason, it was Paul who struck me the most. He sat on the love seat with me sitting to his right on the arm of the love seat.

His hands were hanging between his legs, arms on thighs, head down. I was mesmerized by his tears, huge drops dripping down his face, one after another onto the living room carpet below him, absorbed into the fabric, leaving a dark splotch of wet. He never made a sound except a sniff here and there, but the tears dripped, dripped, dripped, one after another.

Diane and Lee, book-ending Rumer in her usual spot on the couch. Their hands were on her lovingly as Diane whispered to her, "I'll see you again someday soon, Rumer," kissing their hands and putting them on her head.

Rob, finally sitting down next to Paul on the other side of the love seat… my father pacing, pacing, pacing, in the dining nook behind the couch… Cheryl standing next to me on my right.

I started to panic, thinking, "She can't go yet. She's really okay right now, she can make it longer…there's still time to stop this madness." But, then, there comes a point of no return, of going too far to stop the inevitable outcome and we had reached that. I had to quell the panic, thinking of her last few sleepless nights, whining in confusion and pain. I had to think of her.

Rumer looked at us all in turn. I know she understood what was happening. Every time her eyes passed over mine, I smiled at her through my tears with all the love I held in my heart for her. We both knew that we had already said our goodbyes to each other in private. She finally relaxed and Dr. John came back in to give her the last injection, the final bit of pain she would have to feel in her pain-ridden last few years. Unable to bark, her eyes followed him, head resting on her front paws. After the injection, he kneeled in front of her, placed both of his hands gently on her resting head and, voice wavering slightly with tears, recited the Blessing of Animals of Saint Francis. They were beautiful, touching, and kind last earthly words for Rumer to hear. I will never forget Dr. John's decency, his compassionate part in this indecent necessity of life. Thank you again, Dr. John.

As my mother's granddaugher clock struck noon that day, Rumer passed away quietly under Dr. John's praying hands, surrounded by the family she loved and gave life to. Light of my life, my sunshine, my only sunshine, winked out and was gone. My God, Rumer, who will help me sleep now, through this unbearable pain? Who will be my refuge now, when I need it most? Will you ever forgive me? Will I ever forgive myself?

Dr. John left us, and so began the finality of Rumer's physical part in our lives. Cheryl and I went outside with Paul and my father, into the heat and humidity of the quickly darkening and clouding afternoon, evidence of a storm on its way, to begin digging Rumer's grave. We chose a spot on the property not far from my parents' house, outside what we call the "Summer Garden." It is a high point and looks out over our houses, the barn and horses, and road beyond. Rumer loved to lie up on this spot, watching Lee, Diane, or Rob weed and water the garden or to be with my mother as she read in her chair here. From this spot is where she loved to look out and keep track of all that was happening on "her" land. It was a perfect final resting place.

As Paul retrieved his backhoe and began to dig, I walked alone, down the gravel driveway that I had traveled so many times with Rumer, to the barn. So deep in my thoughts, I suddenly realized that I was on autopilot. I didn't hear or smell the nature around me, I didn't see the beauty—not without Rumer beside me. Would I ever be able to again? I had no answer yet, so continued. I reached the barn, hoisted a new bag of fresh shavings on my shoulder, and walked back to Rumer's grave.

When he thought that the grave was deep enough, Paul jumped down into the hole to rake it out nicely and throw out all big rocks so that nothing harsh would touch Rumer's body. He then spread the shavings while Cheryl and I went back into the house to collect everyone. We placed Rumer's body onto a blanket and each grabbed a piece to carry her up the hill to her grave, silent pall-bearers.

Her toys came with her and were handed down to Paul first. We also had her "purple plate," the healing plate Lee had ordered for her, and placed that in the grave, too. Rumer's body was then carefully lowered down to Paul, who gently placed her on her bed of shavings, amongst her toys. I watched as he adjusted her head and body so lovingly to make sure that, even in death, she was comfortable. The last act before covering her was adding my mother's letter to the grave. She was still crying, worried because she wasn't finished writing what she wanted to write. But, she came to the realization that she would never finish. What we all had to say to Rumer was endless. She finally folded up her papers and gave them to Paul to place gently under Rumer's head.

I think that it was the hardest thing I ever had to do, watch as Rumer's grave was filled with sand and dirt, but I made myself stand there, stoically watching every scoop fall. Just as we finished, the first drops of Hurricane Ivan began falling. I felt the breeze pick up and turned my face to its persistent caress, facing the coming storm.

How very fitting…for the next few days, in came the winds and rain of Ivan, but even the fury of the hurricane couldn't quite match the fury of my grief.

AFTER

Love of my life, you are now gone from It. What will my life mean without you? You taught me so much, will I remember it all? You won't be here anymore to remind me, to keep me in line, to keep me on the path of goodness and kindness and love. Your body is not here to hold, your head to smell and kiss, your sideways glance and "harrrrr" to warn, your presence to worship. In honor of your life, I can only aspire to be 1/10th of what you were, 1/10th of your considerateness, your selflessness, your pureness. If I can achieve this small measure of you, I might become a good person.

CHAPTER 47

Who would have thought there could be an "after?" Life without Rumer...? Unimaginable, as life always seems after losing someone dear, someone so important that they have become a very piece of one's essence. How can that now missing piece be replaced, how can the hole that's left be healed, rebuilt, filled?

While our lost one can never be replaced, I found that we do begin to heal again, given enough time, maybe not perfectly nor in the same way, maybe the essence is different, skewed, scarred, and, of course, changed, but it does heal. Even if we might still constantly look, search, for that missing piece, "phantom" pain. Life does go on, yes, but it's never the same. The geese still come and go, announcing their passing with great honking noise, the swallows still swoop in every spring with their excited joyful chattering, the ducks still nest here. I still find myself thinking, "Rumer would have loved this!" when we have new construction on the property, workmen always her desirable obsession for play, or when I experience anything new that I wish I could share with her. Number 8 still runs with Rumer's last tennis ball in its cupholder, now old and "fuzzless" with the years, but no one is willing to remove it—remnant of a life still missed.

After Rumer's passing, Lee told me that she occasionally heard Rumer's bark, an echo from beyond, blessing her with the sound that we all so missed.

Me? I have to admit I was so disappointed. I really try to be open to spiritual awareness, to the possibility of other realms and phenomena, to signs from the beyond. I wished for something like this to happen to me, a small sign that Rumer might still be here, still around me, a part of me—a smell perhaps, a whine, the bark Lee hears. I placed my hands over my eyes and squinted into the sunset, searching for her familiar shape, that integral part of our landscape, but all was so empty. She was truly gone to me.

There comes a point one might reach in life, perhaps you know it, have maybe felt it, have maybe even reached it yourself, when you've finally had too much. And, once this point is reached, you forever after are overly sensitive, overdone, and cannot take any more. For instance, pain. When there's been too much of it in life and you've borne it oh-so-stoically up to this point, thereafter even a little bit of pain is incomprehensible to bear, any slight displeasure unimaginable. Everybody's "point of threshold" is different, but mine was finally reached.

I always had a high tolerance for pain: able to bear all the childhood animal tragedies; the braces that were pounded on my teeth at 11 years old, cemented on one by one, the pain so great that the tears just silently rolled down my face and into my ears while I lay there uncomplaining; the detached retina in 3rd grade and the ensuing 5-day stay in the hospital, alone with patches on both eyes, unable to get out of bed, having to live inside my head in order to stand this incarceration; the family problems and tragedies; my best-friend-in-the-world's suicide at 32 years old; my mother's surgeries... all borne so well. Now, I finally reached my threshold, the ache in my heart so painfully powerful that it felt like a true physical malady, something from which I couldn't possibly recover.

I now found myself crying at everything, things I normally wouldn't, feeling sympathy pain at the mention of something sad or someone else's tragedy, unable to bear even the physical pain that I could have easily borne in the past. The whole next week after Rumer's passing, on vacation, I cried at the drop of a hat. Getting Chinese food that weekend, crying, not able to swallow, thinking how much Rumer loved it. Getting in bed every night to watch TV and crying because Rumer wasn't there, a great empty hole where she always lay between Cheryl and me. And, trying to sleep with no soft, contented, relaxed snoring to lull us...the silence was deafening.

Lily came to bed as usual. We felt her coming up Rumer's dog ramp, her weight causing the bed to bounce slightly to her gait. She took to sleeping in the crook of my arm in between Cheryl and me where Rumer had normally slept. I cried at this, at her sweet purring, paws neatly tucked under her white bib, winking at me as she dozed, a smiling source of comfort even in her own grief of losing Rumer. I'll never forget this kindness from Lily. I hope I am as giving to her since I know that she still, 3 years later, misses Rumer. We realized, especially in Rumer's last few years, the very special bond they shared.

That fateful weekend after Rumer's passing, Cheryl and I walked up to my parents' house Sunday morning, the usual routine we did with Rumer, now without her. Everyone started crying anew, so much so that Lee apologized. Each thing done without her was now a milestone to get over: the last time I did this, Rumer was here.

My mother and sisters visited that next Monday night to see Lily, making it a point to show her extra love and help her through her loss, all of us crying because they would usually have Rumer in tow, bringing her back home. They were nice enough to say that night, "Why don't you two go away on vacation somewhere. Just get away and we'll watch Lily and Cesa." But Cheryl and I were too devastated to do so.

And, perhaps this wasn't such a bad thing for me, this sensitivity to pain. I was so used to not crying, my whole life spent holding back the torrent. Now, I even dreamed of crying, great heart-wrenching sobbing, uncontrollable, sometimes waking me, tears fresh on my face and pillow. I dreamed of my lost loved ones... dreamed they were back from the dead. I'd be surprised and overjoyed in my dreams to have found them again, to have them back. Sometimes, I dreamed that I was hugging them so tightly, hugging a solidness in my dreams that I could never regain in real life. Weak with love and relief in their embrace, I'd sob in their arms, murmuring how much I've missed them and how much I love them.

There was just One of whom I've never dreamed, the One I wished I could dream of most of all.

Rumer was unique. Her life, her essence...we will never have again what we had with her—I will never have it again. I know that's true of any new or different situation, any change, any death, since not only is it the love but it's the history and the life experiences that have accumulated and are now gone forever. But, Rumer truly was a once-in-a-lifetime... experience. She was a change of life, she was a philosophy unto herself, she was a teacher to the living. More profound than any religious figure, a greater life teacher than any philosopher, my personal

Buddha, Rumer taught us all so much about how to live and how to live well, with generosity, bravery, kindness, passion, patience, and love. She was responsible for the vow I took: from now on, my loved ones will never feel anger from me or disarray in their lives because of me. Life runs out on us much too quickly and we end up not appreciating what we have, the present and future that are here for our shaping, for our living. She taught me that I have everything I've ever needed right in front of me.

Because she loved me with my faults, despite my worst and most terrible "sins," she taught me how to forgive. With her unconditional, unwavering presence and love, guiding and gently leading me like an endlessly patient guide dog, she brought me down that most difficult and bumpy road to the final brilliant destination of self-forgiveness and self-acceptance. She showed me how to free myself from qualities that breed turmoil, anger and strife. I could now move forward to live my life in a way as to have as few regrets as possible.

So, with my heart full of love and forgiveness, I "saw" all of this. I understood these life-altering teachings and, ultimately, what life means to me. I realized that I didn't need to see or sense those physical signs in order to prove that Rumer was still around me—that bark, the infamous "harrrrr," the smell of baked pork on a hot summer's day that was *her*—because she is a part of me, a part of all I do and think and live and am. There is no greater sign or gift than this. I could go on.

Cheryl and I, during that next week's vacation, searched for a headstone fitting for our Love, our Life Teacher. We finally found the perfect one, a natural, river-washed stone marker that we engraved with the sentence, "We love thee so, Angel Pie," what I said to her every night before bed.

And, there was one more essential act that I had to perform in order to complete my path toward healing. Dr. John proved to be a vital piece in the puzzle of our life experience with Rumer. The gratefulness we felt toward him couldn't be conveyed with words, but I did try with the following note to him:

Dear Dr. John,

We need to let you know how thankful we are for all you've done for us and for Rumer throughout her life- especially, this past year through her illness. I hope you realize how grateful we are for having you as our Doctor. It's because of you that we were able to care for Rumer much longer than normally possible. It's because of you that Rumer was able to live her final days and minutes at home. And, it's because of you that Rumer was able to have a peaceful passing in her favorite spot surrounded by those she loved most and by those who loved her most.

We love and will always love Rumer—it's been so hard. She was so "big," her presence so great, that the void she left in our lives seems of infinite dimensions. She was beautiful inside and out, a soul of such complete and utter goodness that she made us better people. Nothing can ease the pain of everything that's happened. But, having you as our Doctor, knowing you were there for her and us, allowing us to care for her at home, and seeing the kindness of your heart gave us such peace of mind. Rumer meant the world to us and for the help and kindness you gave her, we are forever indebted to you.

We just want to make sure you know we're grateful for what you've given us all.

Rumer was our "Angel." We would ask her, "Rumer, wherever do you keep your wings?"

Thank you, Dr. John, for allowing our Angel a beautiful life and gentle passing with us.

Thank you from the bottom of our hearts,

Jolene, Cheryl & the Mercadantes

Both Cheryl and I freely admit it…we did everything wrong with Rumer. After her first year or so when we stopped taking her to see Ma in the nursing home and didn't have to drive to my parents' house any more, Rumer was never leashed and never wore a collar. She was never walked outside the property or taken for drives unless the drive was to get her to the vet. She was allowed to manipulate every situation, winning more often than not. She was never socialized, not taken to one obedience class. She was treated as our equals, our daughter, niece, granddaughter. She was fed with a fork and we certainly gave in to her every demand. I'm guilty of this, as are we all. While Cheryl and I made sure we didn't make these same mistakes with our next puppy, did it all really matter? Yes, Rumer was afraid to leave the yard, but her life was so full, she didn't care to leave. She had everything she ever wanted right there in front of her…as did we.

Chapter 48

Cheryl and I returned to work after our week's vacation. Life went on, but it was difficult for both of us. We were lost. We returned home to Lily, the house so empty without Rumer's presence. Lily, starved for love and attention, greeted us at the door, yowling at our feet, Cheryl and I tripping over her whenever we turned.

Neither one of us wanted to mention it, but we found that both of us were thinking the same thing: should we get another puppy? The joy in our lives seemed to be hiding on us. Would a puppy help bring that back? The horror of what Rumer endured in her last few years held us back. I couldn't stand the thought of seeing someone we loved so much, so young and strong and proud at one time, be reduced to such pain, such deterioration, such indignity again. And, I did not want to dishonor Rumer's memory by "replacing" her so soon.

But, the hole she left, the emptiness, was too great. We were both so despondent at its depth that we realized that the joy had been worth the pain. I would rather have lived with all of the goodness and happiness she made for us than without. We did not want to replace Rumer, we just wanted to experience joy again in a different way…We started looking for a puppy.

Because of Rumer, Cheryl and I knew we found the one and only breed for us. Pit bulls are so special, we didn't even seriously discuss another breed. My whole family felt the same, my mother recently telling us with great feeling, "Jolene, Cheryl, thank you both so much for introducing us all to this beautiful breed! I love them so much!"

So, Cheryl and I searched, surfing through pit bull websites for the next two weeks to see if any puppies caught our attention. I also frequented a local shelter to see if any pit bull puppies were available, with no luck. Between Cheryl and I, we sifted through hundreds of websites, weeding it down to 5 or 6 pit bull breeders that we really liked. We just couldn't seem to make a decision.

Finally, one Saturday morning before I left for work, Cheryl said, "That's it! Tonight, when you come home, we are going to go over these last few websites and just decide, just pick out a puppy!"

I felt it, that part of my indecision was due to the weight of Rumer's absence from my life, the numbness she left billowing in her wake. But, I went to work, the fluttering of a little anticipation welling up within me, a slight feeling of excitement for the end of the day to come.

Later that afternoon I was sitting at work, sweater on from the cold that grief can cause, when Cheryl called me. She had been surfing the internet all day again, still looking at websites. "I think I found it. You have to see these dogs!" she yelled in the phone excitedly. She found a website that we had somehow overlooked and she eagerly described the beauty of this breeder's pit bulls.

As soon as I got home that night, she couldn't wait to show me. We perused the site and found the dogs astounding. I felt a tingling, like a limb that had fallen asleep awakening again, and I truly smiled. Cheryl and I, sitting in front of the computer screen, pointing at the parents and then the puppy choices, chattering enthusiastically to each other, knew we found *it*. Thus, Anchor Chain Kennels stole our hearts, a new little chocolate red-nosed pit bull we named Aderyn Hale flying into our lives from Missouri. Another benefit was that she looked nothing like Rumer, although later, after getting to know this little monkey, we found out how similar she really was to Rumer on the inside.

CHAPTER 49

BEGINNING

We drove the 1 ½ hours to Logan International Airport in Boston during October of 2004 to pick up our new baby. Waiting in the cold, austere airport warehouse for her to arrive from her flight, stamping my feet from the cold, breathing out plumes of cold air which brought flashbacks of Rumer's predawn potties as a baby, I was so nervous. I just wanted to see her, to have her in my arms already and take her home.

Suddenly, a shrill beeping of large equipment backing up shattered the muted echoing noises. We looked toward the sound, and saw her. We knew her immediately, able to pick her out from among all the crates of puppies and dogs heading our way on a flat truck. She was a tiny chocolate speck with the white marking on her chest that I remembered from her website puppy picture, excitedly jumping around in her crate, finally seeing *people,* what we learned was her favorite thing in the whole world!

The warehouse workers lined up all the crates by the people who were waiting for their animals. We grabbed her crate and ran to the car. I took her out to inspect her on that frigid October morning. The cloudy Boston sky was spitting drops of freezing rain, whipped into our faces by the ocean breeze, as I clutched my new 7- week-old baby covered in poop. I cleaned her as well as I could but she just wanted to cling to me desperately. I tried inspecting her as we began the drive home, holding her up in front of me as I once held a certain vanilla puppy so long ago, trying to memorize this moment and never forget this beautiful, trusting, living creature, so perfect and healthy, without sores or tumors. We lived with Rumer's illness for such a long time that, my mother, seeing a small bump on Aderyn's puppy body one day, exclaimed in horror, "I know what that is!" She, of course thought it was a cancerous lump. Of course, it wasn't.

It was difficult, though, trying to scrutinize baby Aderyn. She just wanted to be held and close her eyes to finally sleep, so trusting of me to protect and comfort her, waking occasionally to take some food out of our hands and drink some water out of a paper cup. All I could tell was that she had beautiful blue eyes, a red nose and was the stunning color of bronze with a white chest, just like a caramel cream candy.

We reached home and pulled into our driveway to find my mother standing there waiting with such nervous anticipation, wringing her hands with worry. I jumped out of the car and plopped the puppy into my mother's outstretched arms. I watched her face transform from one of sadness and worry to one of such pure joy, laughing as this little baby, covered in poop and the size of a kitten, kissed and kissed this stranger with such wholehearted love. My heart was overwhelmed with happiness.

Aderyn proved to be our healer after the pain of losing Rumer and a bundle of joy equal to no other. Another Savior, she helped deliver us all from our grief. She bore another weight, maybe a different weight, but bore it with the same ease so typical of animals who only want love and to please. My mother, still home recovering from her surgeries, became Aderyn's surrogate mother, "babysitting" her while Cheryl and I worked. Each needed comfort and love, and each gave it to the other unconditionally.

Aderyn was a terrible sleeper at first. She flung herself around in bed at night in discomfort and agitation, throwing herself down, regardless of where she landed. Many times, I awoke at night suddenly, my nose, eyes, face battered by her flailing. This was probably due to her irritable bowel syndrome, which would be another 2 years before we diagnosed and treated it. It didn't help that she lost all her baby teeth at once, too, the bed a bloody, toothy, mess, and contracted puppy warts which transformed her tongue, gums, and lips into topographical disarray. She finally found comfort with Cheryl every night, curling herself around Cheryl's neck as tightly as possible.

Aderyn Hale amazes me every day. From the moment she came into our lives, we always said that she is an old soul. She is so knowing, so smart, so clever, so respectful. Even as a rambunctious puppy, she never ran Lily over or bothered her, almost intuitively knowing that Lily is old. Aderyn is not only extremely respectful of Lily but of all life forms and is nicknamed Aderyn Halo because of her gentleness. She is more apt to watch with a determination to figure something out than to react to a situation, blinking in concentration, eyebrows in a half-circle frown, little girl ears all floppy in front of her face. My mother loves her ears, which grew extraordinarily long, making me understand why her breeder laughed and said, "Well I *guess* they'll be okay," when he had asked if we wanted her ears docked and we said no. My mother tells us, "They look like long, beautiful hair when she holds them behind her as she runs."

Aderyn loves people so much that I trust her implicitly with anyone, young or old. Her favorite thing in life, even more than her ball, is a ride in the car that will take her to meet new people. She is the only dog I know who runs *into* the vet's office to lick and greet everyone there.

The only exception to her overly people-friendly behavior was just one incident with my neighbor. I took Aderyn on the street for a walk one day and saw my neighbor in his front yard. He walked over to chat with me for a while. Aderyn was her usual pulling mess of moving tongue and tail, exuberant in her haste to reach him. Then she noticed another man approaching, who, my neighbor told me, was his brother visiting from the Boston area. Suddenly, Aderyn's head popped up, her long ears in their perked, attention mode, her hair slowly rising along her shoulders as her tail began to curl up and over her back. She squinted at this new person coming toward us, blinked a few times, blew a few huffs out of her nose like a bull, and barked while backing up and jumping sideways.

Completely shocked by her behavior, I quickly admonished her and made her sit like a lady next to me. While she did, she couldn't help the slight whines and wuffs, the soft growls under her breath that kept escaping. Only then did I watch the approaching man, noticing his unsteady, swaying walk and the beer can in one hand, a cigarette in the other.

After our introductions, the man said, "You know," pointing at Aderyn with the hand holding the beer, words slightly slurred, "these dogs are a problem in the Boston area."

Getting a very bad vibe myself, I said, "Oh, really? They're not a problem here and are the sweetest, most loving dogs." Aderyn and I quickly made our escape and, once back in our yard, I stopped to hug her and tell her what a good girl she was and that I should definitely listen to her in the future!

Both Cheryl and I agree, she is the smartest, both logically and intuitively, creature we ever knew. She knows what she wants for an outcome and takes the steps, however many there might be, to get there. She is manipulative to an infinite degree. She is also one of the funniest creatures I know. When she was a baby and we carried her upstairs to bed, her front legs walked in the air as we made our way up, eyes wide open in concentration as she thought that she needed to move her legs even though she was being carried. She barks for her meals if we take too long preparing them, she loves getting behind the pillow cushions of the couch or in my closet behind all my clothes and start barking, making herself sound very far away, she runs like a goof, and she's very uncoordinated except when she's catching her spiny latex football. Catching her ball, she is poetry in motion and she knows it.

She knows how to act cute and play up her sweetness in order to get love. When Cheryl and I come home from work, she stuffs as many toys in her mouth as can fit as she trots around us in happiness. She calculates the best time to steal food at a party, when she knows everyone is preoccupied, pilfering numerous pieces of pizza, sandwiches, or ice cream, jamming her head in Cheetos bags, not caring that the bag gets stuck on her head. She never acted like the "typical" dog, nor does she like "typical" doggie things like bad smells or bodily discharges. If she sees me coming with a Kleenex to wipe her eyes, which gooped up terribly as a youngster, she runs away in disgust.

Aderyn is an unbelievably beautiful dog. She has two colors that vary by seasons, offset by the most stunningly golden eyes. Her summer color is a brilliant gold, as shiny as a copper penny. Her winter color is the deepest chocolate, with flecks of the brilliant gold color of summer highlighting her eyes and ears.

With Aderyn, we did everything right. We took her out somewhere almost every night to visit people, to PETCO, to the library, the nursing home… She met the 100 people they tell you to socialize your puppy to by 4 months old. She went to puppy classes and continued in obedience classes. She went to doggy daycare three days a week from 4 months old to 1 year old, becoming very socialized with other dogs. And, we love doing all of this with her. She has such a joyful and fun spirit that she can't wait to go places and be a part of new experiences.

It's funny how Aderyn seems to know the shy dogs or ones that have problems. She tries to help these dogs and makes it her mission to become their best friend. In Aderyn's puppy class, there was a shy Shepherd who closed herself down to the activities. During free playtime at the end of class, she hid behind her family and stayed on her bed, not wishing to be a part of all the activity and fun.

Aderyn, on the other hand, loved playing with the others and was very social. But, she became fascinated with this cowering, shy pup and began spending less time playing with the group and more time studying this other. She was determined to draw this puppy out and to help her experience the fun everyone else was having. Eventually, as Aderyn persistently kept trying, sometimes following this puppy behind chairs and between people's legs, this puppy began to play! Once she began, she couldn't be stopped. She began to play with all the other puppies as well as with Aderyn. Everyone agreed that Aderyn helped this puppy more than anything else in class and the family always thankfully gave our Aderyn credit for this.

In doggy daycare, she befriended a border collie who was shy and didn't play much with the others. But, after Aderyn showed up, Magic didn't stand a chance. She loved Aderyn and watched expectantly for her every day.

Aderyn loved daycare and all of her friends there very much. Cheryl and I dropped her off before work and picked her up on the way home. She was so excited to go, knowing when the car was approaching the daycare, shaking and whining with excitement to get in and see all her friends. As soon as she entered the building, she walked down the whole fence line licking all the dogs already there. She was very depressed on the days she had to stay home, hanging her head and looking away when we kissed her 'goodbye' and walked out the front door without her.

The owner of the daycare gave us progress notes every once in a while. They're funny when reading them now, revealing how Aderyn behaved. The following are two different "progress notes":

February 4, 2005

Aderyn had a super morning—lots of easy-going play and very respectful behavior.

She stayed pretty calm until just about 11—almost nap, then started to get a little rowdy and over-stimulated. She showed a lot more self-control today and is starting to recall well in the group. She played mostly with Ivy and Basil (boxers) and Abbey (Bernese Mtn. Dog). She practices a lot of submissive/ soliciting behavior with Wolfie (Husky)—he growls at her a lot and is bossy but she worships him.

Heather

July 25, 2005

Aderyn seemed tense about the Boston Terrier today, so I didn't let them play together. She <u>didn't</u> have any outbursts or other behaviors towards him so that was <u>good</u>. I just want to see her relax a little more with him. They did do a short greeting/sniff and that went fine, but I kept them in different groups to play. He left very early, so we'll try again next Monday with this one!

While Aderyn got along well with the numerous dogs at daycare, she did have some favorites: Magic, a border collie; Ivy, the boxer; Morgan, the great dane; and Wolfie, the alpha spitz-like dog who growled at her and told her what to do.

Heather told us that Aderyn had a mutual dislike for one dog: Sully, a Boston Terrier. Although she didn't care for him, she did tolerate him humping her head, as Cheryl and I witnessed on the video monitor in the waiting room when Heather was preoccupied with a phone call. She tolerated this violation with patience beyond her age, hanging her head in submission until Sully was through. I guess I wouldn't have liked him much after that either.

It's funny, though, when Mei Mei came along the next year, how much she resembled a Boston Terrier.

CHAPTER 50

When Aderyn turned one, Cheryl and I thought about getting another puppy. Aderyn is just so fun-loving and social that it seemed she was missing a crucial ingredient in her life. As a good friend of ours once said, "A dog might seem happy and as if they have everything they need but, without another dog in their life, someone who understands them, they are always missing that little bit more."

Once again, Cheryl started looking on pit bull websites for babies. I was very surprised, actually, that she was the one looking. It is usually I who like to have new babies all the time and would have a houseful of animals. Cheryl has even cut me off at times, telling me, "No more— not even a goldfish!"

As I lay in bed reading and watching TV one night, Aderyn contentedly chewing her bull stick on the bed next to me, Cheryl informed me that she found a little female pit bull baby that we had to have. She had passed it by my sisters first a few days earlier, and both were excited by the idea. That night, she pulled up Mountain Creek Kennel's website and said, "Come see this baby—we just *have* to save her."

In came little 8-week-old Mei Mei, deformed tail and all, so very strong and brave to fly to a family where another dog already "owned" everything. Cheryl and I drove to Bradley International Airport in Connecticut on our vacation in September 2005 to pick her up. She came to us with the baggage, confidently looking out from a crate full of toys and puppy things, so surrounded by comfort from Missy of Mt. Creek who was such a pleasure to deal with. As soon as we got her in the car, I took her out of her crate to hold her up, as I once did with Rumer and Aderyn, to look over her perfect black and white body marred only by a kinked tail. Her puppy head was beautifully chiseled with a face that was half white and half black, the eye on the white side rimmed with a thin line of black as though bruised, her right ear pointing forward, always, her eyes the most beautiful color of dark chocolate, as dark as ink. Then she opened a mouth lined with black, making her look just like a geisha with dark lipstick, and I saw her teeth. I exclaimed to Cheryl, "She has demented teeth!"

Laughing, we kissed and hugged and loved our new baby, bonding immediately to her.

When we brought her home, we made sure that we introduced her to Aderyn properly. Aderyn immediately adopted a very kind alpha role, a perfect role model and protector to Mei right away. Mei certainly didn't need protecting. She proved to be a confident, strong little girl with an attitude. Aderyn was fascinated by this little bully that came to stay. She adjusted her play to fit Mei, lying on the floor most of the time when Mei was so little so that she didn't crush her, allowing Mei to use her as her personal mountain to crawl on. Never possessive of anything herself, Aderyn was surprised by Mei's possessive qualities, Mei always feeling the need to "resource guard" her toys and crate, gently shouldering Aderyn or Lily away from her "things" if they headed in their direction.

Cheryl and I discussed the whole puppy routine again, planning to bring her to puppy classes and obedience, as we did with Aderyn. But suddenly, we heard from people that it had been a bad idea to get another female, that females don't get along.

Once again, Cheryl and I researched. We came across some terrible information, some from trainers we knew, some from the internet. A few of the statements we ran into were: "Oh, never get 2 females. They'll never get along"; "Never leave 2 pit bulls alone together. They'll tear each other apart"; "Never leave pit bulls in the house with small animals, like a cat" … We were completely confused and upset, our joy utterly demolished. We went so far as to almost send Mei back to Mountain Creek Kennel in our turmoil.

Partly due to all of this negative advice and partly, for each of us, different reasons, Cheryl and I cried for three days after Mei arrived. Cheryl's reason, as she informed me, was that she didn't think she could love another puppy as much as she loved Aderyn. She loved Aderyn so much that she didn't think there was enough room within her to love another so completely. "How can I possibly love another puppy like I love Aderyn?!" she wailed to me in complete misery. "We have to send her back," pointing at Mei, refusing to use her name for fear she would become emotionally attached.

The only one who was finally able to reach Cheryl and help her through this trauma was my mother. As one who raised five children, she gave Cheryl the best advice. As Cheryl, heartbroken, told my mother her fears, my mother said to her, "Oh, no, after the first baby, it doesn't matter how many there are. A mother's love is more than enough to go around, to have for all her children, no matter how many. You love them all the same—you just do. They just become like one in your eyes." This struck Cheryl to the core. She was finally able to move on, free to give Mei all the love that she held within her.

For me, I was devastated over the fact that we changed Aderyn's life so drastically. We stopped taking her to daycare since she now had a sister at home. What if she missed daycare? What if she missed all her friends, the routine, and wanted her old life back? I couldn't stop crying over this dilemma, Cheryl's misery impelling my own. Now, we had everyone telling us that two females will, most likely, not get along.

My sisters walked down the driveway to our yard to visit the third night we had Mei, so happy to come see Aderyn and the new baby. I was outside visiting with them, Cheryl walled up in the house in her misery, when I had an almost unheard-of breakdown. I am still able to see their faces so clearly as their expressions turned from joy to troubled shock to confusion, staring at me as I burst into tears in front of them, a pretty good rendition of wailing myself. "We don't know if we're going to keep her," I cried of Mei. "We're probably going to be sending her back!" crying as I almost never do in front of them.

I told them how Cheryl felt and how hard it was for us to adjust to a situation that was so different. They were so sweet and supportive, telling me to just see how everything goes, that everything will work out, give it time…me stubbornly unyielding in my resolve that it wouldn't.

So, we both cried, remnants of grief over Rumer and the life of familiarity that we once had with her, I'm sure, the majority of all our heartache and anguish.

Again, we should have asked Dr. John first and foremost. When we took Aderyn and Mei to see him at the end of that week, we told him our concerns. He, totally oblivious to everything we had been going through, said factually, "Of course 2 females would get along the best. They understand each other. It's proven that 2 females will get along best, better than any other pairing."

Again, do I have to say how much I love our vet? Due to our trust in him, his information stated so simply, Cheryl and I put our concerns to rest and began to enjoy the two of them, once again.

CHAPTER 51

Aderyn and Mei are now soul mates. They each know what the other is thinking and know what will set each other off, playfully pushing each other's buttons all the time. I can actually see the wheels turning in Aderyn's brain as she often thinks of different scenarios in order to tease Mei. She knows where Mei hides her stash of bull sticks throughout the yard and knows that Mei hates when she goes near them. She will not bother with them unless she wants to start trouble. When she does, she parades by Mei's hiding spots, tail curled over her back in a teasing fashion, and starts to dig up Mei's "goods." This drives Mei insane. She runs over to Aderyn, tap dancing around her, front feet beating frantically but not willing to challenge her "alpha." Aderyn especially likes to do this when she's outside and Mei is inside, knowing Mei is watching her through the window. Aderyn makes a great show of finding Mei's things and digging them up on her, shaking Mei's treasured bull sticks once she unearths them, all floppy and green from ripening underground, while Mei goes crazy in the house. She also undresses Mei when they have their winter coats on in the yard, ripping the flaps of Velcro in great "teeeeaaars" as they run in play together.

And, Mei, to get her big sister going, runs at Aderyn playfully and stops in front of her, pushing the toy she's holding at Aderyn. She then runs away with a great burst of speed and comes round to Aderyn again, asking to play. Aderyn looks the other way and ignores these pleas until she thinks enough time has passed where it has now become *her* idea to play. Then, the game will be up, both running around their beautiful yard together, stunning in their joyousness. At night, not able to see them, we can only hear the galloping of eight paws on the grass and a "hah hah hah" from Mei as she passes us, breathing in effort while running after her big sister. In order to tease Aderyn, she steals Aderyn's coveted spiny latex football (sometimes the aunties will help her, which she knows they'll do, and watches patiently for their handoff). She then runs around the yard with moves of the best running back ever, Aderyn not able to catch her.

Aderyn and Mei couldn't be more different. Aderyn is big, has a body to die for, and snores like a chainsaw when she sleeps. She is such a kind, sweet soul. She trots in circles around the house when Cheryl and I come home, tail wagging frantically, Mei closing her eyes to its battering as they pass, ears in an ecstatic tight tortellini curl. She bore all of Mei's puppy aggressions, her neck a crisscrossed map of scabs and tooth marks from Mei's teething period. She hardly ever corrects Mei, who can be very pushy, but when she does, it's long overdue and Mei will submissively bow to Aderyn's leadership. Ad's such a gentle soul, such a goofy priss, it just makes us laugh when she does something "dog-like" or "tough" like barking at something or digging up an old disgusting treat.

Aderyn is also our clown, our goof, always trying to get a game going or cheer everyone up, including her sister. She is the peacekeeper, never wanting anyone she loves to be angry and I find that we even have to be careful of our thoughts since I know she can read them. She is intelligent beyond measure and would be a phenomenal chess player if she were a person. At the same time, she likes to be babied, too. When she was little, Aderyn would sit in my lap facing me, paws around my neck, and kiss me softly. Though too big now, she still tries, paws on my shoulders, kissing as she looks lovingly into my eyes, her eyes crossed with the effort. We think she looks like Barbra Streisand. She often sleeps in between my pillow and Cheryl's. I am sometimes woken up in the middle of the night by her kisses, just a few soft, sweet kisses to let me know how much she loves me before sighing, smacking, and settling her head against mine to go back to sleep once again.

Mei Mei is an eternal baby, pushing her head into your chest if she is sick or needs comfort, even doing this to Dr. John one visit when she was sick, forcing him to hug her. And, she's the most joyous creature I ever knew. As she trots around her yard, she just skips with her back feet out of nowhere once in a while, just because she's so full of joy. Cheryl recently told me, " Mei's the best example of 'living in the now' that I've ever seen. She's full of joy every minute of her life."

Mei also has the funniest habit of balancing on her front feet. If she smells something she likes very much, or dislikes very much, up go her back feet. If it's only a "good" smell, not a "great" one, you'll see one back leg start to lift. When she was little, she sometimes balanced on her front feet to eat! Our little circus monkey!

Mei, similar to Aderyn but much more gentle (I call Aderyn my 'Wild Child' since she's full of drama and exuberance), sits in my lap like a baby, a paw on each shoulder to hold me still while she kisses and kisses. When I show signs of getting on the floor to sit so she can get in my lap, she hops around me in great anticipation and throws herself onto my lap as soon as I'm down. She kisses for as long as it's allowed, squinting into my eyes with love. She chooses love and attention every time over food or treats.

Mei Mei is not only our little love, but the best hunter, catching moles that have made our back yard a total disaster and killed some of my beautiful plants. She's like a cat in her patience, spending hours on "mole patrol." She thought she did a bad thing the first time she caught one. She showed me, took me into the back yard, to the place where the mole was lying on its back, little legs curled in the air, stiff in death. At first, I didn't see what Mei was trying to show me, so she kept rubbing me and walking to the spot. I finally spotted it, all sopping wet with saliva. Although I felt bad, I praised Mei, who was acting quite upset, not sure if she did the right thing. After I praised her, she ran around the whole yard with joy, flinging a toy in the air as she went.

Mei's the only dog we've had who actually cleans herself. She spends hours at night, cleaning her paws one by one, making sure to get in between each and every toe, cleaning them until her white is as brilliant as my childhood collie's. She looks like a typical "old time" pit bull, as if she should be sitting on a milk wagon with a man, both smoking cigars as they make their deliveries all day together. She loves all the "doggie" things: eating green, moldy 'goods'; rooting around her yard; hunting; barking in protection… She trots through puddles with uncaring abandon while Aderyn daintily and prettily prances like a show dog around anything dirty or wet.

Left alone in the house with Lily all day, they are so good with her. They defer to Lily every time, recognizing her as the "elder". Even at the water bowl, where Lily tends to dwell drinking for long periods of time, the two of them, Ad and Mei, wait in line behind her for their turn to get their drink.

Although completely different, these two comfort each other, love to make each other laugh, sleep with each other, play together, share things, and kiss. Their love for each other could not be more profound.

CHAPTER 52

When Mei was 6 months old, we had her spayed. We were informed that she also needed her tail removed since it was arthritic and painful to her, "the worst deformed case" the veterinarian surgeon had seen in a tail. Two weeks after her spay while Cheryl and I were on vacation, we brought her back for her tail surgery. We picked her up that afternoon after getting the call that her surgery went well.

When they led Mei out, I had to stifle the gasp that tried to escape. I hadn't realized what Mei would look like immediately following the surgery and was saddened by the shaved butt, the complete loss of anything remotely tail-like, the discomfort she was in. We took her home and gave her the medication Dr. John sent with us, but it didn't touch her pain. I called Dr. John back and informed him of Mei's condition. He promptly called in a stronger prescription for her to the Brooks Pharmacy in our town. Cheryl went to pick it up while I stayed with Mei, very concerned about her level of pain.

By 8:00 that evening, her pain was so intense, even this stronger medication didn't help. I stayed up most of that night with Mei as she paced the house, crying in pain. I'll never forget the sound she made. It was a soft howl-cry, "whowoooo, ouooooo," a sound I never heard from her before or since. Cheryl and I gave her more and more medication until finally, at 3:00 am the next morning, she curled up with Lily and me on the living room floor in a pile of blankets and fell into an exhausted sleep. For those people who claim that pit bulls are "impervious to pain," I can tell them that I wouldn't wish it upon anybody to have witnessed Mei that night in the pain she was in. She was very sick for a few weeks after this ordeal and broke out in sores, her immune system so compromised.

Thank goodness that Cheryl and I have both Aderyn and Mei on the raw food diet. I think this helped Mei get through her surgery as well as she did and what keeps them both healthy. Although I researched the raw food diet thoroughly, I still worried that we might not be doing it correctly, that we might not be giving them the proper nutrition and vitamins that they need. Rumer's early onset of arthritis was still so prevalent in my mind as something I might have caused.

Dr. John came to the house one sunny spring afternoon to give the horses their annual checkup and shots. While standing with him in the barn that afternoon, the rays of the sun warming us through the open barn doors, the swallow couple swooping in and out over our heads, I hesitantly broached this subject. I, still so pained by Rumer's loss, said to him, "I don't know if I did enough for Rumer," my voice cracking with pain.

I can still see his reaction, in all his generousness and sweetness, not understanding my full meaning, the guilt that I still bore, the profoundness of my pain. He stopped what he was doing, turned to me so quickly that his hair fanned out around him, and exasperatedly said, "Of course you did! How could you even think you didn't do enough for Rumer?"

How could I convey to him my guilt, explain my feeling of complete failure as a mother? I quietly and stoically accepted his kindness, his absolving me of my faults, his uncomplicated statement putting it all in perspective for me. I still tell him every once in a while, just so he never forgets, how much I appreciate him. He is a rare and wonderful person indeed.

CHAPTER 53

It is true what some people say: not everyone should have a pit bull. But, this is because not everyone deserves to have them, not everyone deserves to be in the presence of these angels, certainly not those who abuse and try to make them some extension of a macho fantasy. They are unlike many other breeds. So sensitive, they live to please their beloved person/s, and they expect to be a part of everything you do. They are such a dichotomy, so very strong and powerful, yet the most easily upset breed I know. I thought that my collie was sensitive, sensitive to moods, scoldings, and reprimands. But the pit bulls that I've had and known have all other breeds beat. Training methods that might work for other dogs often fail miserably with pit bulls. People are the most important thing in their lives and they are crushed if they think they've disappointed anyone.

My Aderyn, who, if you were sawing her leg off, would lick you while you did it, refused to go with one trainer during an obedience class. This was after the trainer used a harsh method to try to stop her from pulling on the leash. Thereafter, Aderyn dragged the trainer back to where Cheryl and I sat, shutting down completely if the trainer asked something of her. She was so startled and upset at what the trainer had done that she turned her back on a *person*, something unheard of with Aderyn.

Mei Mei, as well, always and forever the baby, having to suckle herself to sleep with a soft toy, is very upset if she even senses my mood is sad or angry. She sometimes carries this into the next day unless we properly put her at ease.

Pit bulls have a sweetness, a connectedness with the human being that gives them an understanding of us that's almost scary. On our commutes to work together, Cheryl and I inevitably start talking about our girls. We always start with Aderyn and her funny behavior and the intelligence and sweetness that define her. And then we tend to dwell on Mei and exclaim, "Where did she ever come from? What a character!" She is just so indescribable that everyone seems to say this of her, from her miniature pit bull body, to the chestiness she got from her father, to a split, extra big front tooth, to her tailless back end. Cheryl, in talking about Mei and all of these traits of hers, said to me on one commute, "She's a little light in my heart." How sweetly put and how true of her place in our lives.

Mei and Ad continue to give us the joy that Rumer gave us every day. Because of Rumer, we now have these two beautiful souls to continue her unbelievable legacy. I don't know what I'd do without them. When I take Aderyn and Mei for their daily walks around the property, we occasionally find one of Rumer's old tennis balls, all dirty and aged. Aderyn and Mei sniff it indifferently, if they even notice it at all. I wonder sometimes if they can smell Rumer on it, if they're aware of the soul of one who was so loved, as they are now. I wish I knew.

Both of them, Aderyn and Mei, have such different lives than Rumer did, as do we with them. I find myself thinking quite a bit about this as I sit here, looking out my back bay window, drinking my coffee at the dining room table. I'm lost in thought, aware that Addie is standing out in the yard, visible through the window, staring out over the fields as she watches our family of wild rabbits play in the gathering dusk. Mei's inside with me, her front half lying on her cushioned bench in front of the window near me, her favorite spot to look outside from the safety and comfort within. I feel as though I'm in a time warp, that I will see Rumer walk by any minute, sniffing through the sunflowers under the bird feeders, meandering her way across the fields, slowly poking her way to Grammie's. The past and present weave in and out cruelly, my brain knowing it can't be true, but my heart, that magician of dirty tricks, makes me think Rumer is back and living amongst us again. My heart sometimes breaks for what used to be.

Then, a thought surprises me out of this reverie, Ad and Mei in front of me, once again, "So, this is how it is for people who have dogs, this is the 'normal' life with dogs"... still so used to Rumer's "human-like" behavior. Although Ad and Mei are different, this doesn't change the fact that their essence, their qualities, are the same as the ones Rumer possessed: loving, considerate, knowing, understanding, and oh-so-funny. And, my heart breaks in a different way, breaks for how so very much I love them. No, Rumer was not a "fluke" in the pit bull world.

My mother has since retired from her job and "babysits" Ad and Mei every day that Cheryl and I work. People are, many times, surprised that my mother is willing and able to babysit two pit bulls. If they mention this to her, she strongly lectures them on the true pit bull attributes. Her love for them could not be greater, as it was for Rumer. She then jokes by telling them, "They're my *good* grandchildren."

Every night, Cheryl and I call my mother to see how her day was. We look at each other and laugh since her response never varies, "Oh, Jolene and Cheryl, they are *so* good. I can't even tell you. They do anything I say." Recently, she has added, "They're my best friends, really." They love and adore her to the ends of the earth, respect her, and behave like angels for her.

This is what Rumer has done for us, for me. This is what our pit bulls continue to do. I often hear people spout some gems: "Pit bulls don't belong in civilized society"; "Why would anyone want one, why can't everyone just get a Golden Retriever?"; "The only good pit bull is a dead one." But, they are not monsters. They are not impervious to pain, they are not aggressive, indiscriminate attack machines, they do not "turn" on you arbitrarily. They are loving, kind, considerate, giving, good, and pure living creatures. At the same time, they are dogs. They might not do everything expected of them. They aren't perfect and we can't expect them to be. Just like any other dog, or person, they need to be treated without bias.

Interestingly enough, I find that many pit bulls spend their lives with this realization of how some people think and feel about them. I see, especially in Aderyn, how they constantly try to disprove these unjust, hateful stereotypes by showing as much love for people as possible. Aderyn sometimes goes overboard in her effort to prove her love for everyone. With a total lack of dignity, she, with all humility, acts in the most silly, absurd way, sometimes contorting herself in upside down poses while licking madly to show her loving submissiveness.

I find this sad, this trying so hard to prove themselves. When I talk to Cheryl about this, she tells me that I have to stop looking at it that way, not to feel sad but to be content that they are proving their human-friendly qualities. After all these years, I guess I'm still striving to be more like Cheryl, and probably always will.

Aderyn and Mei continue, for me, the life lessons that Rumer so eloquently taught me. The most important thing is that I am living the best years of my life right now, every minute. They have taught me to not waste any time here with those I love and cherish. In this most profound way, my girls keep everything, all there is to life, in perspective.

And, what Rumer meant to me, all that she gave to me, this slice of happiness and joy in my life, this golden ray of pure sunshine (my only sunshine) that brightened my darkest hours—how could anyone have the right to say she shouldn't have existed, or she should have been euthanized for what she was? It isn't what Rumer was, but *who* she was that mattered. Living with this fellow earthly being was a life-changing event. Rumer's life and the writing of her story brought me on a journey that few have the privilege of traveling. Where would I be now without her, without this golden touch of an angel? One answer, the most important, is that I would not be as good a person today, or keep aspiring to be the person of whom Rumer could be proud. I have come to realize that, because I love her, because I am a part of her, and she of me, so completely, so forever, our love is the connection now, the way I live my life our tangible hold.

Rumer left me with quite a life-fulfilling legacy and a weight on my shoulders equal to that we placed upon hers so long ago. I can only hope to bear it as she so nobly did. To do any less, to be any less, to *live* any less would be a great dishonor to the beauty that was *her* and would prove that her life lessons were taught in vain. I could never allow that.

So, I'm a far better person for Rumer. I'm a far more giving person because of Rumer. When you love someone that much, you don't care what you have to do, what you have to give up, in order to keep them a part of your life. And, if you think you're too tired to give any more, you find that you *can* dig deeper, your love allows it, allows you to reach deeper and find that little bit more to give. You become selfless.

In 2006, two years after her passing, I wanted to immortalize Rumer permanently in a special way. I decided to get a tattoo of her. I chose my favorite picture, one that Dr. Kay had taken on one of her visits to our house. It was of Rumer at about five or six years old as she looked in her prime, an exquisitely perfect specimen, sitting on a boulder, panting her joy and happiness on a beautiful summer's day.

I looked diligently for the right tattoo artist, needing to find one who could do a portrait tattoo. A portrait tattoo is a special art since it is done from a photo and must look like the person or pet. I finally found the right person. She was wonderful enough to work with me since this picture wasn't the clearest, but she knew it meant the most to me. We designed the tattoo with the picture of Rumer, adding the most beautiful wings to her back, the wings of an angel, wrapping around to her chest. I had it tattooed on my left shoulder so that I would be able to see her at all times. She is now, truly and in all respects, the Angel on my shoulder. She not only keeps me on the path of the straight and true, but continues, through me, to educate people who ask about my tattoo, always the teacher.

I love Rumer more than there are words. She was special for all of this revealed here in her story, but for so much more, as well. As with other people who are left to life after someone they loved has passed, there is the thread of that lost loved one's essence forever after between them. This thread holds us together, Cheryl and I, so much more strongly than we were held together before—and, that's truly special.

I don't know what the future holds but I do know one thing for certain: my life will always be filled with peace, love, and happiness as long as I have my loved ones and my animals. My animals complete all that I am and aspire to be because of their goodness. Now, I savor and treasure all my good moments, and those good moments fill my life, for each one might be that one that could change my life for the better forever.

Aderyn, Mei, and I take our daily walks in the fields and I sometimes see the ghost of Rumer as she was young again, that beautiful grounded dolphin, leaping and weaving through the tall grass and purple clover, her laughing face just visible as she runs for the sheer joy and pleasure of it. And, I give my own yell of joy to Ad and Mei and run with them, Rumer's ghost keeping pace, able to laugh for everything they bring to my life. Now, when the pines speak as we run by, I hear the whispers of her love.

As one full day of fun, joy, and love follows another, we, as we did with Rumer for 12 ½ years, pile into bed ("bed and snacks") every night. Before I can close my eyes to sleep, I get up one last time to hug and kiss a snoring Aderyn Halo and tell her how so very much I love her and am honored to have her in my life. I kiss her sweet, precious head and smell her with love, a different smell than Rumer and even Mei, a sweet smell that is unique to her, so fitting for one as sweet-tempered as she whose only mission in life is to love as much and as many as she can. Sometimes she opens one golden eye a slit, letting me know that she hears me.

Then, I crawl into bed, on the sliver that I'm allowed in this king-sized bed, to an awaiting little Mei Mei Olivia. She has been watching me kiss Ad and patiently waits for this moment. She truly believes that I am her Mama. She dotes on me and lives to watch for me night and day. We call her my "little baby" and she believes this to be so. She sighs with contentment that I'm finally in place and curls into a little ball in the crook of my left arm—her spot every night—nudging me to cover her with her special, soft blanket. I tell her how so very much I love her, too, and that she is special as are all my "babies."

And, there is just one last thing of which I can be sure. One might wonder what the face of pure goodness looks like, a face that shines with only true and pure intention, the face of an angel. I can answer that now. I can tell everyone that I know what the face of an angel looks like, for I have seen one. She has a full black muzzle with black whiskers, a little white on her chin, and the most beautiful and loving soft brown eyes shaped like almonds and surrounded by black mascara applied just right. She might be marred in appearance by two missing bottom teeth in an otherwise perfect, brilliant smile. Her ears might be stinky at times and darkly stained with dirt from a good day of rolling in unmentionables, but her soul is only light.

I love thee so, Angel Pie.

Epilogue

"**Doesn't** it give you the willies?" the library patron I was helping asked. He was talking about my life with my pit bulls. While I was checking his books out for him, he noticed my tattoo and asked if it was a Boxer. I said "No, Rumer was a pit bull." He grimaced and shook a little as I explained that I live with two other pit bulls now, thus, the question. So, I patiently went into my speech about how pit bulls are actually one of the least aggressive breeds toward people, make poor guard dogs, and are absolute loves. He listened politely and added some things himself, like, "What, it's when they're in the wrong hands then?" I smiled and said, "Partly."

I keep educating. I am tireless in my passion and more patient with this than with anything else in my life. There isn't an hour that goes by at my work place that someone doesn't ask about my tattoo and, most of the time, I have to admit that people are understanding and supportive of pit bulls and have much empathy for the abuse they oftentimes endure.

But, it's people like that man who shivered at the mention of a "pit bull" that keep propelling me on my mission. It's this kind of person, especially this kind of person who might also hold office and support Breed Specific Legislation, or might be a veterinarian who allows his/her biases to interfere with treatment, or a potential adopter that passes by the innumerable pit bulls in shelters who so desperately need adoption... It's this person who needs to hear Rumer's story. I do not believe that one could hear her story and still feel that way when confronted with the words "pit bull."

There are so many good people out there fighting to stop animal abuses of all kinds and many people, many whom I know myself, who are fighting for these dogs. Although I am an advocate for all animals and strive to help stop all cruelties and abuses, pit bulls can become a passion, a way of life. They certainly have for me. Rumer was unique in the way we lived with her, yes, but she was not unique in the sweetness and gentleness of her soul which **IS** the pit bull.

MYTHS:

- **Bred to be aggressive.** Pit bulls were originally bred as rat dogs. They would be placed in a pit with rats to see how many they could kill. People eventually began to fight them with other dogs. In order to handle a dog in a fight, the dog had to be especially NON-aggressive toward people. Throughout their history, the people- aggressive gene has been bred out of them.
- **Impervious to pain.** Pit bulls feel pain as do any other creatures. As a matter of fact, they are cold in the winter, hot in the summer, their feet cannot take the ice and they are sensitive to emotional pain as well as physical.
- **Bred to be a protective breed.** Pit bulls were never bred to be a protective dog. They actually make very poor guard dogs and, very often, go off with a stranger because of their overly-friendly nature.
- **Pit bulls have more bite pressure per square inch than any other breed.** Both German Shepherds and Rottweilers have stronger bites.
- **Pit bulls have locking jaws.** There is no such thing.
- **Pit bulls cannot be trusted around other animals or children.** Pit bulls live in peace with many other animals and dogs. They were actually nicknamed "the nannies" because of their known love for children, so much so that they would be babysitters to the family's toddlers. Their love for children is so well-known that it is a part of their listed breed characteristics.
- **Pit bulls will suddenly "turn" on beloved owners.** This is a complete legend that was also said about the Doberman in the 1970's when the Doberman was the victimized breed at that time.

ADDITIONAL FACTS:

- Breed specific legislation (BSL) is a law that different communities try to pass which bans certain breeds of dogs from those communities. If passed, it affects family pets that have never done anything wrong. It gives the authorities the right to go to people's homes, take their dogs, and euthanize them. When this happened in Denver in 2004, people formed an "underground railroad" in order to help save their beloved pets and get them out of the city to safety.

- BSL can include such breeds as Rottweiler, Chow, Akita, German Shepherd, Doberman, Presa Canario, Mastiff, American Bulldog, Bull Terrier, Shar Pei, Siberian Husky, Malamute, Great Dane, Irish Wolfhound, Scottish Deerhound, Cane Corso, Belgian Malanois, Tosa Inu, Dogo Argentino, Canary Dog, Perro De Presa, Neopolitan Mastiff. (www.understand-a-bull.com)

- A recent study of 122 dog breeds by the American Temp. Testing Society shows that pit bulls have a passing rate of 83.9% and higher. This rating is better than collies (79 %) and Golden Retrievers (83.2) and is 4th highest overall.

- Pit bulls serve as therapy and service dogs- Neville, a bomb sniffing dog for Seattle, WA serves where his breed has been banned!

- Petey on Little Rascals was a pit bull. America's first war dog, Sergeant Stubby, was a pit bull and the most decorated dog in military history and the only to be promoted during battle.

- Helen Keller's service dog was a pit bull, Sir Thomas

- Popsicle, a rescued pit bull, is the 1st US customs dog. RCA is a certified hearing dog in Alaska. Tahoe, Cheyenne, and Dakota are search and rescue pit bulls that worked at the World Trade Center after 9/11. Wallace the pit bull was the 2007 National Frisbee canine champion.

- Many celebrities have pit bulls: Rachael Ray, Cesar Millan, Jon Stewart, Michael J. Fox, Serena Williams, and Pres. T. Roosevelt had one, as well.

- Many home insurance companies will not insure people with "dangerous dogs" including pit bulls. Many charge an exorbitant fee if they do.

- Media has had terrible bias against pit bulls, rarely reporting the good pit bulls do, yet report so much of the negative. In addition, the media rarely reports when other breeds bite.

All of this is discrimination. Dog facilities that will not accept pit bulls or won't allow them in their businesses, or just making owners with pit bulls muzzle their dogs before walking them in certain areas or vet clinics. This is all prejudice and based on the breed and not the individuals.

WONDERFUL WEBSITES:
- http://animal.discovery.com/tv/pitbulls-and-parolees/
- http://pitbulls.iwarp.com/photo.html
- www.badrap.org
- www.wallacethepitbull.com
- www.cesarmillaninc.com
- www.la-spca.org
- www.understand-a-bull.com
- www.theunexpectedpitbull.com
- http://fataldogattacks.com
- www.realpitbull.com
- www.blackbeautyranch.org
- www.bestfriends.org
- www.shortywood.com/pitrescue.htm

ADOPTION SITES:
- www.petfinder.com
- http://adoptapet.com
- http://www.pbrc.net
- http://www.outofthepits.org
- http://www.bull911.com/pitbullrescue.php
- www.animalfarmfoundation.org

SOURCES:
- Badrap.org
- Realpitbull.com

ENDNOTE:
Although I stated that I have my dogs on the raw food diet, it has since become imperative that I switch their food to a kibble-type food. Aderyn has irritable bowel syndrome and could not handle the raw food diet. While it works for many dogs, some cannot tolerate it. There are many good sources that give information on the raw food diet and rate and analyze regular dog foods. Informing oneself is only a part of making decisions on what your dog eats. The most important part is your dog him/herself. As with people, what works for one does not necessarily work for another. Now, however, at least we have a choice of some very good quality dog foods on the market.

DOG FOOD ANALYSIS SITE:
- www.dogfoodanalysis.com